Leading and Learning in the Workplace

Learners are always motivated; they just may not be motivated to learn what you want them to. This book shows leaders and trainers how to foster learner engagement in workplace training contexts, using the powerful construct of motivational immediacy.

Not only does this book counter learner resistance from a positive and holistic perspective, but it also puts forward the unique perspective that every act is a learning act for those being led and a teaching act for those leading. Since learning and leading are linked at the core, the motivational immediacy framework serves to keep learners engaged, instructors relevant, and leaders understanding and effective. Based on robust theory and research, this book defines motivational immediacy as both a phenomenon and a practice, offering concrete action steps that will enable leaders and trainers to:

- Maintain motivation on a regular basis
- Distinguish between true engagement and resistance when learners argue
- Find common ground with students
- Realize that instructors do not teach groups, but individual learners who may sometimes be clustered together
- Develop the habit of "reaching for" instead of reacting, running, or repeating when choosing a response to any situation, and more.

Addressing leading and learning in an entirely new way, this book will appeal to workplace training providers and directors, course designers, administrators, supervisors, and leaders at all organizational levels.

Jonathan E. Taylor is Professor and Director of Doctoral Studies in Adult Education at Auburn University, USA.

Leading and Learning in the Workplace

Exploring Motivational Immediacy

Jonathan E. Taylor

Routledge
Taylor & Francis Group
NEW YORK AND LONDON

Designed cover image: Getty Images Cecilie_Arcurs

First published 2026
by Routledge
605 Third Avenue, New York, NY 10158

and by Routledge
4 Park Square, Milton Park, Abingdon, Oxon, OX14 4RN

Routledge is an imprint of the Taylor & Francis Group, an informa business

Library of Congress Cataloging-in-Publication Data
Names: Taylor, Jonathan E., 1972– author
Title: Leading and learning in the workplace : exploring motivational immediacy / Jonathan E. Taylor.
Description: New York, NY : Routledge, 2026. |
Includes bibliographical references and index.
Identifiers: LCCN 2025025479 | ISBN 9781032772424 hardback |
ISBN 9781032764399 paperback | ISBN 9781003482079 ebook
Subjects: LCSH: Organizational learning | Employees–Training of |
Employee motivation
Classification: LCC HD58.82 .T394 2026
LC record available at https://lccn.loc.gov/2025025479

ISBN: 9781032772424 (hbk)
ISBN: 9781032764399 (pbk)
ISBN: 9781003482079 (ebk)

DOI: 10.4324/9781003482079

Typeset in Galliard
by Newgen Publishing UK

To Debbie, who enters every space with a visible nimbus of energy, kindness, and love.

Contents

Section I

Street-Smart Motivation

Understanding Motivational Immediacy

Chapter 1

Becoming an Expert

Leading and Learning in the Workplace

In everyday language, we tend to think of expertise as the consistent ability to do something exceptionally well. And, in everyday living, this sort of thinking serves us well enough. For those who wish to *be* experts, however, it does a disservice. In seeing expertise this simplistically, we tend to seek it ineffectively. To speak of expertise as the capacity for and habit of exceptional work is to focus on the outcome of expertise rather than the substance. It tells us what it results in but doesn't answer the question of just what might give life to the result; what might cause it.

For those who wish to be an expert in workplace leadership and training but do not yet feel as though they have reached it, the important thing is to learn what constitutes expertise – what one can do to grasp it and use it in the furtherance of life goals. We do need to know the outcome of expertise just like we need to know the outcome of eating or drinking, but simply knowing what expertise is as a final product does not help us prepare the meal we wish to enjoy.

The question of what constitutes expertise is not a new one, and although there have been many nuanced views of it over the years, the most widely accepted empirical view of expertise is wrapped up in the ability of an individual to have a deep, conceptual understanding of a process, system, or domain and to apply it in creative ways in novel situations to solve problems and produce positive outcomes.[1] Systems thinking, that is, seeing all the parts of a thing clearly and in relation to one another, is a key element, as is the ability to imagine novel solutions to problems that arise.

This book is about learning and leading at work. It is about the indelible connection between these two dynamics. This book is for those who wish to become experts or to increase their level of expertise. It is for those who like the idea of stepping out in front, working with purpose, and getting things done. Mostly, it is about doing these things in such a seamless way, and with such quality, that it overflows into the lives of those around you

DOI: 10.4324/9781003482079-2

and makes them want to follow your leadership in hopes of getting more done, being better at what they do, and, in a small way at least, becoming more like what they see in you.

The key to becoming a powerful learner, teacher, leader, and mentor, is *Motivational Immediacy*. Understanding what motivational immediacy is, how you can achieve it, and how you can bring it to bear on your daily life goals will open new pathways for you to increase your intentionality and success, whether you are on your first day on the job as a line worker, or in your 20th year as a CEO.

Motivational and Leadership Principles

Motivation is *not* your friend. In fact, it is responsible for every weakness you have ever struggled with and every failure you have experienced. It may be that the only thing more harmful to you in your working (and personal) life than motivation is the way you have been conditioned to think of motivation in the first place. The most dangerous enemy is, after all, the one you think your friend.

Motivational immediacy has lots of moving parts but also has an intuitive clarity about it once it has been explained and evidence has been provided. Overall, it is a simple concept, though it has many different domains through which it can be applied. It is built upon a great deal of empirical work from a number of different academic and professional disciplines. Of course, motivation is responsible also for all of the good and best accomplishments in our lives, but we are fully aware of those. It is the sinister side of motivation that we studiously ignore.

Given all of this, the following pages are intended to share the concept and then provide practical ways forward and concrete actionable steps for improving your ability to learn, lead, and provide mentoring and instruction in the workplace. Since every efficient and effective "do" thing is brought to life by a well-thought and understood "think" thing, the concept will be introduced as the foundation for action. Motivational immediacy has nine fundamental principles upon which effective practice rests, which will be briefly addressed after a word about the relationship between teaching and leading.

Lead Like a Teacher; Teach Like a Leader

Every act in life is a teaching act.[2] The things one does are experienced by all of those around them. These experiences always "teach" either consciously or unconsciously and result in downstream behaviors, psychological habits, and practical outcomes.[3,4] The implications of this truth are significant. If leading others is about teaching them (albeit, perhaps, informally providing instruction to them through action), then the most profound learning theories and practices apply to leadership as well as teaching.

The point of bringing the concepts of workplace training and leadership into the same space is to highlight the overlap that exists between them and to bring the strengths of each to bear on the practice of the other. The fact of the matter is that very often, both leaders and training instructors in the workplace see educating and training as a mostly classroom-oriented transmission of information and knowledge, and leading as either something more formal than it is (being the boss) or more informal than it is (the person everyone looks up to in the office).

In reality, each has something the other can learn from and by looking at them side by side, the capacity and reach of both can be empowered and extended. And, in those cases where there is a significant overlap, both leading and teaching will be fostered with more power. A continued mantra throughout the book will be: *Lead like a teacher; teach like a leader.*

To be clear, anytime I am addressing what I have experienced to be prevalent attitudes or behaviors in the workplace, I do so with humility. I realize that what I am saying doesn't apply in all situations or to everyone, but I am writing with the intention of helping all of those involved in each of these activities be more of what they would like to become as the even better versions of themselves.

Motivation Is Bi-Directional

Human beings are motivated to do good things and to do bad things. Likewise, human beings are motivated to learn and they are motivated to *not* learn.[5,6,7] Common parlance in the instructional world is to talk as though learners are either motivated to learn, or not motivated to learn (i.e., in a neutral state waiting to be motivated in the right direction). This is not an accurate way to think of motivation and it will reduce the efficiency of both leaders and instructors to think so. Learners may be motivated to learn, but they may also be specifically motivated to not learn. This latter state is common in the workplace and its existence has significant implications for how we address those around us in learning situations.

> *Motivation is a moment-by-moment dynamic, and it is the responsibility of the effective instructor/trainer to work to tap into the employee learner's motivation during every moment of the learning event.*

Just because adults are "motivated" to pass a training course, get a workplace certificate, or even learn something from a specific training course, does not mean that they are motivated in any given instant to learn a particular thing, at that particular moment, on a particular night, etc.[8,9] Therefore, the instructor/trainer must work to make every moment an engaging moment and simply cannot "clump" the employee–learner's motivation around more global concepts such as "I want to have a certification for future promotion," "I want to be a forklift operator," or "I want to be an officer in the USAF."

The learners who argue the most with you may be the learners who are the most engaged, rather than the least engaged.

While persistent, inappropriate, and disruptive arguing can certainly be an indicator of learning resistance, persistent argument from an employee–learner may often be a sign of true engagement rather than resistance.[10,11] Resistance is a failure to engage[12,13] (not a failure to accept, per se), and well-reasoned argument over training content (or, perhaps, policy) is typically a sign of active engagement with the learning experience. This distinction and how to parse it from resistance and use it for the benefit of the instructor and learner is a vital skill for the practitioner.

If you are not truly interested in the class/content you are providing instruction for and don't think it is authentically important for your students, they will not think it is interesting and important either.

In talking to leaders, teachers, and trainers throughout the years, it is very often the case that they are stuck sharing a policy, or teaching a class that even they see as a "waste of time" or "not that important." In these cases, the leader who wishes to be highly effective absolutely must first find a way to find value in what is being taught him or herself. Failure to do this will, at best, result in an inefficient motivational context and at worst be evident to the learner. The very best way to motivate students is to be authentically motivated as a teacher first, and then work with learners to find the common ground.[14]

An instructor/trainer never teaches groups. An instructor/trainer only and always teaches individual learners who may sometimes be clustered together in groups.

Concepts of group and organizational learning will not be contradicted in a theoretical sense in the book, but in a practical sense, practitioners will be challenged to understand that "speaking to the middle" or "teaching to the center" is not an effective tool for those who wish to rise over and above average and be highly meaningful teachers.

Understanding and paying attention to learning resistance is a very learner-centered approach to teaching.

Understanding and analyzing the learning resistance dynamics at play in any given instructional experience is one of the more learner-focused approaches to teaching and instructing. An approach to training that takes learning resistance into account is a learner-centered approach that (a) meets the learner where they are; (b) empathizes with the learner; (c) collaborates with the learner to address the learner's conceptions, perceptions, and positionality; and (d) takes the learning journey with the learner.[15,16]

In order to understand adult learners fully and to bring the most comprehensive conceptually-based expertise to bear on fostering learning engagement in the workplace, practitioners must expose themselves to an interdisciplinary, cross-theoretical body of literature and research.

Workplace training and development, as a field, has often been self-limiting in theoretical scope, particularly with respect to the motivational theory and science of mainstream educational psychology. All practitioners who deal with learners of any age absolutely must be "well-read" and "wide-read," and this book will provide the framework for that necessary exposure.

Employee learners resist for many different reasons, but the behavior manifests itself in many of the same ways despite being the outworking of different causes.

Because resistance behaviors and cognitions are often manifested in the same ways despite having different precipitating causes, leaders must work to understand the complicated reasons why employees may be resisting so that they do not apply a "one-size-fits-all" remedy.

In every area of life, each day, we are faced with situations that require a response. In these situations, we can either engage in a reaching for, reacting to, running from, or repeating of.

Reacting to, of course, is highly susceptible to emotional, ill-thought decisions that have significant repercussions, some of which may be long-term. However, the classical notion of responding instead doesn't ensure that we will make good decisions, even if we think them through. There multiple ways one can respond and not all of them are equally beneficial. If we are not aware of the different "go-to" respond options we commonly use, we are apt to fall short of optimal practice. *Running from* is an easy option but also one with significant consequences for our work, relationships, and successes. *Repeating of* is the ultimate act of powerlessness because we end up making decisions that have already been shown to be harmful, that we have not chosen for ourselves, and which erode both personal agency and productive power. *Reaching for* is a habit that can be developed and results in an intentionality and freedom that can result in innovation, success, and positive personal health. One can either select from these four options by rote or can choose to make decisions that form behavioral habits for life.

Motivational Immediacy

Motivational immediacy is an expansive construct that is connected to formal and informal teaching, and importantly, also to formal and informal leadership. In both of these two significant categories, it has inward-focused and outward-focused concerns (Figure 1.1)

With regard to workplace instruction, the inward domain of motivational immediacy refers to inward phenomena of both the leader–teacher and employee–learner. It refers to a moment-by-moment feeling of motivation on the part of the *learner* to engage in the learning opportunity directly at hand. This is in contrast to long-term, or non-immediate goals, such as retirement, and future promotion.

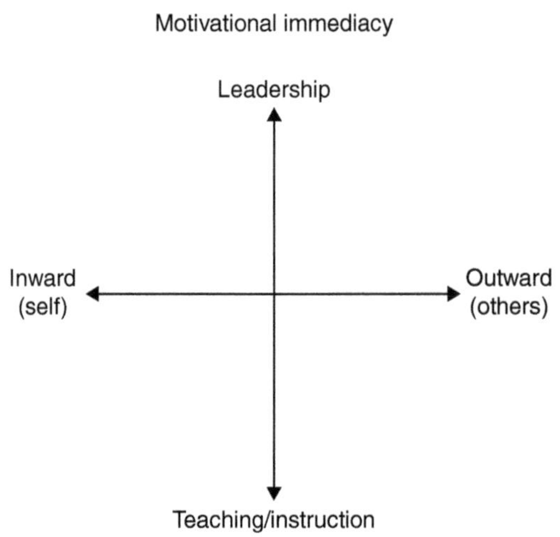

Figure 1.1 Motivational Immediacy Domains.

Outwardly focused, as a practice, it is the instructor's process of working to stay relevant and foster engagement consistently at every moment of the leading and teaching activity rather than relying on global motivators such as future promotion, and second careers.[17,18] These global or long-term goals are not a negative drag on learning, but they lack the power to consistently drive necessary engagement behavior day-to-day, in the moment.

Applied to leadership, motivational immediacy also takes on both an inward and an outward domain. Internally, motivational immediacy is learning to "reach for" the long-term goal with each short-term decision. It is the mental process of thinking of long-term goals and forcing oneself, as a habit, to connect each short-term action to that long-term goal in a way that mentally "fuses" the means (short-term action) to the end (long-term goal). This purposeful act of *reaching for* is an alternative to other mental habits such as *reacting to*, *running from*, and *repeating of. Reaching for* is a term that I have used to refer largely to the academic theoretical term *Means-End-Fusion* (MEF).[19]

Externally, motivational immediacy is leading others with an understanding that every act is a learning act for those being led, and therefore, every act is also a teaching act for those leading. The highly effective leader will understand that every decision, every policy, and every new idea will result in learning on the part of those experiencing that leadership, and because of this natural dynamic, each decision, policy, and new idea is teaching someone something. That *something* will work itself out in practically harmful or helpful ways in the workplace environment. Again, it is connecting in a thoughtful but habitual way the short-term act with the long-term goal.

In support of this leader/learner-centered approach, the dynamics involved in learning resistance will be addressed thoroughly in the book, but from a positive perspective. Learning (training/leadership) resistance will be defined as a *failure to be open* to learning in a given context. It will be addressed as a problem faced by the employee–learner rather than a problem faced merely by the instructor or leader, *with* the learner. Learning engagement will be defined as the *mobilization of internal resources* (emotional, psychological, cognitive, and physical) for the purposes of learning.[20,21,22] Taking these concepts together, each as the opposite of the other, will allow for a candid discussion of the problems faced in the training classroom and the workplace by the leader–teacher and employee–learner alike. A foundational premise of the book will be that the instructor/leader–learner interaction is fundamentally a collaborative effort, and because of this, any problem faced by the one will be faced, quite naturally, by the other.

The book will provide a comprehensive conceptualization of learning engagement and learning resistance in the workplace, is multidisciplinary, and will draw from fields such as Adult Education, Workplace and Training

Development, Psychology, Educational Psychology, Sociology, Cultural Anthropology, Communications, and Leadership. Using those literatures, it will present a comprehensive explanation of leadership motivation, but introduce it from a novel perspective, using everyday parlance.

Structure of the Book

Because the best *doing* things typically follow the best *thinking* things, the following chapters are organized to provide this experience for you. Many authors encourage you to skip around and "cherry-pick" chapters you would like to read. I encourage exactly the opposite. I do hope you could benefit by reading any of the chapters in any order, but I encourage you to be patient and read them in order. Expertise is about a deep conceptual knowing that results in a consistent practical application, so learning about the ideas I am sharing is best done by working first to understand the conceptual foundations of the idea and then seeking to understand the many ways the idea can be applied. This book is practical, but like all of life, is moving along practically only in so far as it is headed in the right direction in the first place. In that sense, the why precedes the how, and for good reason.

Accordingly, the book is divided into three sections:

Street-Smart Motivation: Understanding Motivational Immediacy
The Expert Leader and Teacher: Practicing Motivational Immediacy
Navigating Complications: Motivational Immediacy in the Real World.

In Section I, the concepts of motivational immediacy, learning resistance, learning engagement, and effectual learning will be addressed in clear, practically oriented ways. These constructs provide the foundational principles that build the cultural and interpersonal conceptual understanding that allows the workplace leader to practice with a high level of effectiveness and efficiency. Each of these concepts is addressed in terms of their applicability for the workplace leader, training director, and training instructor. The interconnected "underneath" of these roles is woven together in the four chapters of the first section.

Chapter 2 provides information on street-smart motivation and how having an empirically informed understanding of motivational concepts can improve practice at the street level. It is theory with teeth.

Chapter 3 provides a detailed overview of the dynamics involved in workplace learners being motivated to not engage in provided learning opportunities. It represents the significant portion of learning motivation in the workplace but is studiously avoided in most positive books on workplace leading, mentoring, and training. It is, however, a deeply learner-centered area of focus and will provide the means to extend the reach of any instructor, leader, or mentor in any workplace setting.

Chapter 4 draws all of the threads together from the first section and provides an interwoven concept of leaning and motivation in the workplace. It is the culmination of these concepts and provides a detailed description of the concepts of motivational immediacy and effectual learning that will serve as the foundation and backdrop of Section II.

Section II moves to action. It begins with the theoretical and drives it directly into practice. Chapter 5 takes on the leadership role and provides practical strategies, tactics, and techniques for becoming a more powerful leader in all domains of personal life and the workplace.

Chapter 6 asked the question of "what are we doing here and where are we doing it?" Chapter 7 digs into the instructional learning space and looks at the practical ways to engage in workplace leading, mentoring, and instructing. It discusses conceptual frameworks, leaner storyline, and dialogue as the true ways to foster authentic, long-lasting learning in the workplace. Chapter 8 really digs into the street-level work of the classroom in addressing instructional methods and lesson plans that reflect motivationally immediate methods that will captivate the heart of learners across the organization. Chapter 9 wraps up Section II by sharing some detailed ideas and guidelines for designing curriculum in the workplace and addressing common pitfalls to avoid when doing so.

Section III speaks to the many concerns that the critical eye will have had for the claims and practices shared in the first two sections of the book. Those who have minds prone to play the "devil's advocate" and those who have been around for long enough to know that the world rarely provides our well-thought plans with a fair playing field will be able to explore the real-world obstacles that must be overcome in order to practice and "live" motivational immediacy in the workplace.

Chapter 10 provides a frank analysis of face-to-face and distance learning and how motivational immediacy principles are best applied in these different domains. The decision of whether to have on-site or distance learning opportunities is complicated and fraught with potential legal implications, and this chapter provides some guardrails for making these decisions.

Chapter 11 discusses measurement. Measurement has become a driving force in all learning organizations, and this chapter provides a framework for how to measure some of the more qualitative aspects of motivational immediacy practices. Chapter 12 discusses ethical issues that arise with these concepts and a potential way forward for dealing with some of the more prominent issues that may be faced in the workplace. It examines some of the ethical dilemmas that instructional experts often face in the real world.

Although it is likely impossible to avoid all of these situations in practice, the chapter provides some suggestions for reducing the tensions that arise in these situations.

Chapter 13 draws all of the threads together from the entire book; provides an overview of the concepts, implications, and practices that have been described in the previous 12 chapters; and provides a challenge to try new things going forward. There is no progress without courage.

This book is about motivational immediacy, effectual learning, leadership, and teaching, and how all of those things can be brought together for a more powerful learning and growing organization. I have previously written two academic books and a number of journal articles and book chapters that deal with some of these core constructs and how they are applied in higher education and the workplace. The great majority of this book is original and is addressing either new things or addressing them in a very different way. Additionally, this book is written to be more approachable and more easily applied to the real-world workplace. It is important to note that the concepts of motivational immediacy and effectual learning, the learning efficiency index, the facilitator as mediator (FAM) model, and a few other concepts are not new ideas and they do appear in these previous works. There is no overlap or very little in most chapters, but a few chapters (6, 7, and 11) do have some noticeable overlap, with permission, from the previous two books.

A Word about Theory and Method

First, a word about method. One of the significant criticisms lofted at theory is that it is too abstract and therefore not helpful when one is attempting to enact change in the everyday lived experience and what we call "practice." It is not only theory, however, that suffers from too much abstraction. It may be surprising to hear that methods are frequent fliers in the world of abstraction. It makes sense that theory would be abstract, but in many ways, the exact opposite is true – theory is often practical, and methods are often abstract. *That* claim has likely never before been made in print.

First, both theory and method can be used in abstract ways, or in very concrete, context-specific, practical ways. Using either one in a purely abstract way may, for some, be fun, but is not practically rewarding for those who, once again, are trying to get things done. Anything randomly applied to any context without any contextual or conceptual linkage is, in essence, an abstraction. For instance, if you go into a grocery store and give a lecture in the frozen food aisle on physics, you may be saying great stuff, but your act will be a completely abstract event for everyone there who is simply trying to find something for lunch or dinner, which is everyone else besides you.

On the other hand, if you are giving a lecture on physics at any place where people have, in one form or another, signed up to learn about physics, your lecture has a chance of being practical – at least in so far as it succeeds in allowing those who hear it to successfully check the box they were trying to check. It is practical in so far as it is purposeful, contextually relevant, and achieves some concrete goal for someone. In this sense, theory can help someone achieve an entire host of practical goals, while a random method often won't.

This example demonstrates a principle that is not often spoken of – *whether something is practical or abstract depends largely on the context in which it is introduced.* Concepts like abstract and concrete, theoretical and practical, are contextually bound.

Instructional methods (and leadership methods as well) applied without any forethought and intentionality are purely random, badly limited by context, and in the end, mere abstractions. Here are some examples:

- Leading an icebreaker at a staff training event without knowing precisely what the purpose of the icebreaker is, and how it will improve the educational aspects of the event.
- Using PowerPoint to share "rote" information to a bunch of employees who you want to start behaving in a particular way *even* when you are not looking.
- Showing up early to the office and leaving late *just because* you read about it in a book and someone told you it would set the right tone (it may or may not depending on where you work, what the job is, and in what specific way you think it will change your colleague's behavior or attitudes in concrete ways).
- Kicking off employee award programs in the office without finding out first whether or not that particular type of thing is valued by those working there.
- Taking down the walls to everyone's workspaces because that is "all the rage," and is what will allegedly help everyone work more and feel better.

One thing that should be recognizable in reading this list is that all of these things may in certain contexts be good things and also practical things. Here is the key – what makes them *abstract* is the blind application of them to any given context without understanding WHY they are good for WHAT you are specifically trying to accomplish in your particular WHERE and at your particular WHEN.

What is the takeaway here? The only methods for any kind of practice that are practical and concrete are those which are connected to conceptual and theoretical understandings on the part of the leader and teacher, and those which are purposefully applied to a situation in accordance with that knowledge. Any method that is employed without any understanding of the conceptual and theoretical reality from which it is birthed, is abstract and, if successful, will at best be a lucky accident and at worst a physics lecture in the frozen food aisle.

The Challenge

There is a gauntlet thrown here. We are all very busy. There are many "great ideas" being thrown at us online, in advertising campaigns, and in the bookstore. The question before the discerning mind is always, "is this worth my time?" To this, perhaps oddly, I would say – it depends. For those intending to simply scan the text or try to snag a few applicable bits out of a chapter or two, maybe-maybe not. But for those who are intent on learning, for those who are intent on grasping hungrily at truths that will propel them forward into greater ownership, intentionality, success, and influence, the answer is a simple, but resounding yes. Authentic learning requires authentic engagement. Given that, the challenge for those reading this book is to read it critically. That is, think of what the ideas would look like in your particular context. As you read about each concept, think about what it means for you, specifically in your world, and as you consider each application, think about what sort of practice you might adopt or modify in the everyday working life you experience. Ideas are only as good as they are contextualized to very specific human lives and very concrete human action. I can elucidate concepts and I can provide examples of applications, but only you, the reader, can conjure the highly contextualized practical actions that are presently needed. You are already a professional and an expert if you are taking the time to read books in an effort to improve the power of your reach. In that sense, I know, I am preaching to the choir. We get out of a thing what we put into it. I encourage you to throw yourself at this activity for all your worth. Then, you can be assured of coming out of it with wisdom beyond that which I have provided in the following pages. Think of what you want and think of how each idea in this book could help you get it. If you read with this energy, commitment, and thought for tomorrow, you are being motivationally immediate.

Notes

1 Swann, R. H., Plummer, K. J., & West, R. E. (2020). Toward functional expertise through formal education: Identifying an opportunity for higher

education. *Education Tech Research Development*, *68*, 2551–2568. https://doi.org/10.1007/s11423-020-09778-1

2 Taylor, J. E., & McKissack, J. (2014). Zones of intervention: Teaching and learning at all times and at all places. *International Journal of Vocational Education and Technology*, *5*(3), 21–33.

3 Taylor, J. E. (2021). *Motivational immediacy: Fostering engagement in adult learners*. Stylus.

4 Taylor, J. E. (2022). *Motivational immediacy in the workplace: Facilitating learner engagement in training environments*. New York.

5 Taylor, J. E. (2021). *Motivational immediacy: Fostering engagement in adult learners*. Stylus.

6 Taylor, J. E. (2022). *Motivational immediacy in the workplace: Facilitating learner engagement in training environments*. New York.

7 Taylor, J. E. (2014). Starting with the learner: Designing learner engagement into the curriculum. In V. C. X. Wang & V. C. Bryan (Eds.), *Andragogical and pedagogical methods for curriculum and program development* (pp. 55–80). IGI Global. https://doi.org.10.4018/978-1-4666-5872-1.ch004

8 Taylor, J. E. (2021). *Motivational immediacy: Fostering engagement in adult learners*. Stylus

9 Taylor, J. E. (2022). *Motivational immediacy in the workplace: Facilitating learner engagement in training environments*. New York

10 Taylor, J. E. (2021). *Motivational immediacy: Fostering engagement in adult learners*. Stylus.

11 Taylor, J. E. (2022). *Motivational immediacy in the workplace: Facilitating learner engagement in training environments*. New York.

12 Taylor, J. E. (2021). *Motivational immediacy: Fostering engagement in adult learners*. Stylus.

13 Taylor, J. E. (2022). *Motivational immediacy in the workplace: Facilitating learner engagement in training environments*. New York.

14 Frye, S., Taylor, J., & Stafford, A. (2017). The first fifteen minutes: Learning engagement, learning resistance, and the impact of initial teacher-student contact. In C. X. Wang (Ed.), *Theory and practice of adult and higher education* (p. 342). Information Age Publishing.

15 Taylor, J. E. (2021). *Motivational immediacy: Fostering engagement in adult learners*. Stylus.

16 Taylor, J. E. (2022). *Motivational immediacy in the workplace: Facilitating learner engagement in training environments*. New York.

17 Taylor, J. E. (2021). *Motivational immediacy: Fostering engagement in adult learners*. Stylus.

18 Taylor, J. E. (2022). *Motivational immediacy in the workplace: Facilitating learner engagement in training environments*. New York.

19 Kruglanski, A. W., Fishback, A., Woolley, K., Belanger, J. J., Chernikova, M., Molinario, E., & Pierro, A. (2018). A structural model of intrinsic motivation: On the psychology of means-ends fusion. *Psychological Review*, *125*(2), 165–182. https://doi.org/10.1037/rev0000095

20 Taylor, J. E. (2021). *Motivational immediacy: Fostering engagement in adult learners*. Stylus.

21 Taylor, J. E. (2022). *Motivational immediacy in the workplace: Facilitating learner engagement in training environments*. New York.

22 Marks, H. M. (2000). Student engagement in instructional activity: Patterns in the elementary, middle, and high school years. *American Educational Research Journal*, *37*(1), 153–184.

Chapter 2

Street-Smart Motivation

There are two main principles addressed in this chapter. The first is that street-smart experts understand the concepts and tools they work with, which in this case is human motivation. The second is that street-smart experts work with motivational *fields* rather than motivational factors. Each of these principles will address motivation from a direction significantly different from the mainstream, and each of these principles can make a very noticeable difference in how effective you are as a leader, a mentor, and a teacher.

Sorting Ourselves Out on Motivation

Most of us are aware of two very different kinds of knowledge. On the one hand, we are aware of the more intellectual sort of knowledge, often referred to as "book smarts." On the other hand, we speak of what is often called "street-smarts." The words we use for these two types of knowing convey the aspects, for better or worse, that we all intuitively see as connected with them. To be book smart is to be full of accurate, true, and reliable information, albeit information that is not always seen as being very useful for everyday life. To be street-smart, however, is to possess a much more practical knowledge. It is also accurate and true but known more for the work it gets done; the things it accomplishes with "boots on the ground."

In a strange sort of sociology, because of our tendency to categorize knowledge like this, any given person also tends to characterize knowledge about any one particular ***domain*** into these two categories, each owning its own properties. For instance, if asked the right questions we would likely be able to share some basic facts about the Sun – (a) the earth circles the sun (b) when our side of the earth is facing the sun we have daytime (c) the sun is much bigger than the earth (d) the sun is a long way away from the earth, and so on. None of this information is tremendously helpful to us

DOI: 10.4324/9781003482079-3

on a day-to-day basis, however, and we have a parallel stash of knowledge about the Sun that we use more often and with better outcomes – (a) it is difficult to see when the sun is in our eyes, (b) the sun will damage our skin if we don't protect it, (c) the sun will damage our car interiors if we don't protect them, (d) sunny days are better at the beach than rainy days, etc.

The big distinction between the first collection of knowledge about the sun and the second is that the second sort of knowledge comes with a variety of *actionable* items. With respect to the second list above, we need to (a) remember to take our sunglasses when we are outside; (b) wear sunscreen at the beach, at the park, or while doing yard work; (c) we need to put the sunshade up in our car before leaving it parked for the day; and (d) we need to check the weather before planning a picnic.

Everything I have described about the way we think about knowing is so much a part of our daily life that we don't focus on it in conscious ways, instead just moving through life somewhat ignoring the former and mostly employing the latter. My point here is not to take issue with the general trend. It may, in fact, largely be a good and useful way to navigate life, or it may be fraught with long-term practical peril, or it may likely be some combination of both. What *is* very important for the topic at hand, is that in the case of our knowing about motivation, we have the book-smart knowledge mixed up with the street-smart knowledge. *We have them almost exactly backwards.*

There is a problem with the way we talk about motivation. The problem isn't about mere wordsmithing, pedantic maneuvering, or academic hair-splitting. Practically speaking, we are being inefficient at best, and often ineffective, by thinking of learner motivation the way we do. It doesn't take long when hanging out around workplace leaders, program developers, and instructors to hear these sorts of phrases – "These learners just aren't motivated!" "I just need to find a way to motivate them," or "This was a great class because these were all motivated learners." The number one question I have heard all around the world when discussing these topics is, "How can I motivate my learners?"

On the surface, these all sound reasonable and it is not easy to spot the problem. There *is* one, though, and once you see it, you can't miss it and will notice it whenever you hear it in the future. The problem is that those statements presuppose that learners are either motivated to learn, or not motivated to learn; that one is either motivated to learn or in a complete stasis – a sort of learning neutrality that requires nothing but a positive nudge to get them rolling.

The fact of the matter is – and by fact, I mean empirically supported information about human learning – all learners are motivated at all times.[1,2,3] They simply may not be motivated to do the thing you want them to do, or think they ought to do, or need them to do. When a learner resists learning in any learning space, they are exhibiting motivated behavior.[4] They are motivated to *not* learn.

Going back to the whole idea of book smart and street-smart, we can see that the two are reversed. When talking in depth to individuals from all walks of life and from all over the world, I have seldom found anyone who doesn't, at least to a certain extent, know that motivation is an emotional drive of some sort rather than a behavioral direction. We tend to know some basic technical facts about human motivation, much like we have a list of basic trivia about the sun. The problem is that the street-smart sort of knowing we have about motivation is the opposite of the street-smart knowing we have about the sun. Our street-smart knowledge motivation doesn't work well on the street, and it isn't smart.

Similar to book knowledge that doesn't seem to have much practical value, our colloquial ways of referring to learning motivation (i.e., "My learners aren't motivated!") make sense to us but don't serve our practice well. They work badly if they work at all. Oddly, our book knowledge is in this case, the street-smarts that we need so badly. Going forward, if I share technical information about motivation or anything else in this book, it is because I think it will help you in practical sorts of ways while engaged in everyday, real-life activities. The rest of this chapter is about reorganizing what we know about motivation and making our street-smarts street-worthy.

Reeve defines motivation both in a technical manner as "those processes that give behavior its energy and direction," and also in a more colloquial sense by saying that motivational study is for understanding why people "do what they do."[5] It would seem then that motivation plays a role in both resistance and engagement. This provides the substance for one of the claims I have promised to make in this chapter – the dual nature of motivation. Simply put – learners are never unmotivated. Instead, learners are always motivated either to learn or to not learn. One must admit that it may be feasible that there may be a technical middle ground where motivational neutrality might exist, but I would also cry foul if too much of a fuss was made about that possibility because it is more theoretical than practical. Students generally have a reason to checkout or to check-in.[6]

Leading through Motivation and Demotivation

Motivation moves us forward toward a particular end. Or, as the case may be, it holds us back from moving toward the ends we might otherwise want or need. Motivation comes in many different forms. We tend to think of motivation as a strong drive to do something. For instance, when someone asks you what your "passion" is, you talk about what motivates you for this or that in life. We think of it as a driving force that makes us, almost naturally, to want to get up and do a particular thing. This is true enough. There are, however, other less interesting, less exciting forms of motivation. We are motivated to get out of bed when the alarm goes off because we want to earn a living and either want to keep the job we have, or in the very least, want to avoid losing it. This drive to avoid a behavior is important and I will return to it later, but for the moment, it is important to identify this sort of drive as motivation, even if we stop short of calling it a passion or drive.

Brushing our teeth might be another motivationally driven activity. In most cases (good for you if you find this a passion), there is nothing exciting about making ourselves stumble into the bathroom before bed and clean our teeth. We do it, at least most of the time, because we are motivated to do it. Although none of us may be willing to admit it, we might be able to look at those rare times when we slap the bedside lamp off absently, without taking care of bedtime routines such as brushing our teeth. It is important to understand that this is also motivated behavior. It is not that we are not motivated to brush our teeth – that motivation certainly runs deep and remains consistent in the general sense, but we are, in those moments, overcome by a greater motivation to go to sleep. Now.

Returning to the idea that we might be motivated to avoid as well as to achieve, and sticking (sorry) just a little longer on the tooth brushing motivational scheme, people are generally divided into two groups on motivated behaviors – those who do something to *obtain* something, and those who do something to *avoid* something.[7] The way this plays out in brushing teeth at night, after a long day, is that Joe brushes his teeth to avoid having cavities, or receding gums, and Amber brushes her teeth so that she can continue to have healthy teeth. This might sound like some sort of unimportant academic hair-splitting, but it deeply important because a great deal of research has shown that those who are motivated to obtain something (called "approach motivation")[8,9] are healthier in a number of different ways than those who engage in "avoidance motivation."[10,11,12] This is important, for the leading and learning sector especially because it means that *simply getting those in the workplace to conform to a certain set of behaviors, does not mean that one is leading in an optimal way.*

If what I am saying here is true – and it is – then there are a few vital takeaways for the workplace trainer, instructor, supervisor, and/or leader.

1. When you want someone to learn something (i.e., do something), you need to motivate them, and you need to *demotivate* them. If you want to be really good at leading and teaching, you can't rely on motivating people to learn, you must demotivate them to *not* learn. Chapter 3 addresses the reasons people are motivated to not learn.

2. If you want to rise above your peers and really excel as a leader and teacher, you must learn to motivate people to engage in *approach motivation* for the mindsets and actions that are required, rather than *avoidance motivation*, even though either one will get the job done in the short term. Excellence, mastery, and expertise are all long-games.

For the remainder of this book, when I use the term motivation without any specific definition, I am using it to refer to an internal, underlying drive that initiates or sustains behavior. When I refer to it as an internal drive, I am not referring to what the source of the motivation may be (an internal motivator or an external motivator), rather I am referring to the fact that motivation is an emotional and psychological force and therefore, whatever its cause, is experienced and felt from within the individual.

Demotivation

Earlier on, I made a pretty strong claim that our thinking about motivation was selling us short. The concept of demotivation that I am going to share here and in other places in this book is one example of how more technically accurate knowledge about motivation provides a hard, practical edge. When the word demotivation is thrown out, the thing that comes to mind in most people is the idea of punishment. It is true that our modern sensibilities might have brought us all to a place of feeling some reserve when discussing, and especially applying punishment, but most know that there is a time and place. It takes very little time in any workplace in the world to learn from co-workers which rules are enforced, and which are not. There is a reason that this conversation takes place and it has a great deal to do with whether or not the proper motivational factors are in place in terms of the conduct at play in the discussion.

A proper understanding of motivation, however, can straighten us out on this. Punishment is not *de*motivation. Punishment *is* motivation. Remember the difference between what is called approach motivation and what is called avoidance motivation. Both are types of motivation to achieve something (these constructs belong to a family of theory referred to as achievement motivation).

Take for example a workplace where hardhats must be worn on the shop floor at all times. Suppose an employee named Mike does not like wearing a helmet, especially in locations where he (and to his mind, everyone else) knows there is no real need to have it on. Mike, quite naturally, tends to 'forget' it often when on the shop floor. The supervisor has told Mike a number of times that this behavior has to change – the hardhat must be worn. Up until this point, and with most other employees, various types of subtle motivational factors have done the trick. Doing the right thing is an "oldy but goody." Then, there is the peer pressure of other rule followers doing what is supposed to be done. Trying to please one's employer and supervisors is also often a motivational factor that comes into play. I just provided three motivational factors for Mike to wear the hardhat, but he is very often not doing so. That is because he has at least one motivational factor driving him to 'forget' the hardhat and leave it in is locker again. Either he has more motivational factors driving him to leave it behind, risking the ire of his fellow-workers and supervisors, or he has *more powerful* motivational factors driving him to leave it behind. Either way, the volume and power of the motivational factors driving Mike to not wear the hat outweigh those that might otherwise have driven him to wear it.

Now, suppose that Mike's supervisor, under growing pressure from senior management decides to take action and apply a punishment. The moment the memo is posted indicating that a failure to wear a hardhat on the shop floor will result in a one-day suspension from work, Mike is not Demotivated, Mike is instead exposed to a new motivational factor. The reason this is true is that Mike was never without motivation to begin with. Mike was motivated to *not* wear the hardhat. With the new policy implemented, Mike is now more motivated to wear the hardhat. That is, the motivation to wear the hardhat is stronger than the motivational factor(s) to not wear it. What is important here (and it is very important for the expert), is that Mike was not demotivated in any way, he was motivated *more* to do something else. However, the sort of motivation that was facilitated for Mike was what is called avoidance motivation. That is, Mike is motivated to wear the hardhat so that he can avoid some unpleasant experience. This may, in fact, be an effective strategy for the supervisor, but is likely not an efficient one.

That is because avoidance motivation is a much more problematic form of motivation, and it has negative implications for both the individual being subjected to it and the greater context in which it is being applied. Mike will be more likely to have a tendency to have what is called an "anticipatory effect" that leads toward a "biased interpretation of social information."[13] That means that Mike will have a tendency to anticipate negative consequences whether or not they are there.

Again, for short-term compliance, this will likely be good enough, but leaders seldom are happy with short-term results that turn on them later on. Mike's avoidance motivation will also likely lead him to have lower subjective well-being, which simply means that Mike will feel less happy about his job and also life in general.[14] All of this might seem like someone else's problem to the classroom instructor trying to check-off some learning objectives, or an administrator trying to get employees to stop parking in the fire lane, but for the expert leader and teacher, the long-term subjective well-being of the employee matters and is seen to have a legitimate effect on the health of the organization as a whole.

Having said all of this about punishment being a motivational factor and therefore not representing what I am referring to as demotivation, we are left with the question of what demotivation is. Demotivation is an extremely powerful tool in all spheres of leadership and training, but one which cannot be utilized fully and expertly without a clear idea of what motivation is and how it works. *Demotivation is the removal of motivational factors from the context and experience of an individual or group.* In Figure 2.1, you can see that the motivated conduct, represented by the circle, is being driven by three different motivational factors (those on the left with the arrows outside the boxes facing toward the desired behavior).

Each of these factors can either be an approach motivation or an avoidance motivation. Approach and avoidance valance is represented by the arrows pointing in two different directions. Keep in mind that what we are talking about here is avoiding or approaching some third thing, not the desired conduct itself. For example, whether wearing the hardhat to earn a

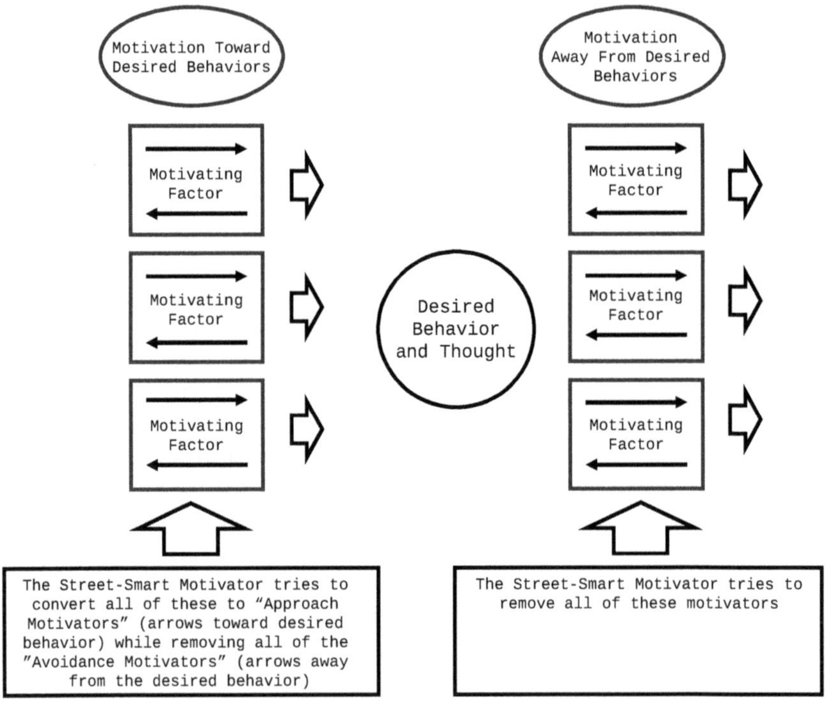

Figure 2.1 The Motivational Field.

supervisor's praise, or wearing the hardhat to avoid a day off without pay, Mike is still motivated to engage in the desired conduct of wearing the hardhat. Mike is not, however, motivated to wear the hardhat for the most efficient and healthy reasons, and those negative reasons will leak motivational efficiency for the organization and whatever service or product it delivers.

Punishment, in this figure, would simply be adding a fourth motivational factor, one that would certainly be an avoidance motivator. Demotivation, on the other hand, is to rearrange the context in a way that facilitates the *removal* or *reduction* of some or all of the motivational factors that are driving a particular behavior. This is not done by providing more motivational factors, but by working to actually remove some of the existing motivators for the undesired behavior. Just how to do this will be discussed more fully later on, but to clarify the point here, in the case of Mike and his hardhat behavior, removing motivators is key. Perhaps Mike is motivated so strongly to not wear his hardhat because the hat is very heavy, fits poorly, and gets in the way of another piece of safety gear he feels he needs more, like hearing protection. Demotivating Mike in this case would include actions like procuring more modern, light (but effective) hardhats, and perhaps finding other forms of protections (e.g., eye and ear) that are compatible with the hardhats. This particular example, of course, comes with a price tag, but there are likely other ways to demotivate Mike's bad behavior that wouldn't cost much. And, of course, it may be likely that it would be worth the cost of new gear if (a) employees started wearing their safety equipment, (b) had fewer injuries, (c) brought fewer lawsuits against the company, and (d) were healthier and happier at work every day while they worked to produce. In fact, one less serious injury and the ensuing legal challenges might make up for the cost. The point here, however, is not about this particular way of demotivating Mike, but about how to work with colleagues in ways that results in more powerful leadership, happier relationships, higher productivity, and a healthier workforce.

Motivational Valence

In addition to motivation and demotivation (adding or removing motivators), it matters a great deal about what sort of motivators an individual is experiencing in relation to a desired behavior. I mentioned a few times already that there are a number of reasons why being motivated to achieve something in order to approach something is better than being motivated to achieve something in order to avoid something (i.e., negative consequence). So, beyond the street-smart motivator's effort to remove motivators for undesired attitudes and behaviors, motivational valence must also be attended to. The effects of this work might be more nuanced and difficult to spot in the short-run, but they will be present nonetheless, and working in this area of the motivational field provides one more area for the expert to have an extended reach.

The section above on demotivation focused on removing the boxes on the right side of Figure 2.1. That is, demotivating involved facilitating a change in the learning/working context so that the motivations to not engage in the desired behavior either went away or became so weak that they were of no effect. In the case of facilitating motivational valance change, it is the boxes on the left side of Figure 2.1 that are of importance. Within each of these motivational boxes, you will see thin arrows pointing both toward and away from the desired behavior. This represents the reality that even though each of those boxes represents a motivation to do a certain thing (or think it), the motivation for doing the thing may be an approach motivation or an avoidance motivation.

Going back to the example of Mike and the hardhat at work, Mike can be wearing his hardhat everyday so that (a) he remains healthy and can return safely to his family each evening after work, or (b) so that he can avoid some punitive action in the workplace, such as the loss of pay for a day's work, or a write-up in his personnel file. Each of these would likely motivate Mike to wear the hardhat and therefore appear in the short-run to be effective. However, they are not equally effective when more factors are taken into account.

There are internal factors that can lead an individual to tend toward avoidance motivations rather than approach motivations, but this can be strongly influenced by the motivational context in the first place. There are various motivational factors in the workplace that can be fostered and arranged in ways that will more likely increase approach motivation and decrease avoidance motivations. Like all of the concepts being covered in this section, very specific attention will be given to the practical ways to actually do these things in the workplace. First, however, it is important to understand them.

A Quick Numbers Game

Application will be discussed more heavily later on, but in the spirit of being 'immediate' here, consider the following example of how this might matter in a workplace learning situation. Figure 2.2 shows the same picture as above, except for two things. First, it has hypothetical weights attached for all of the motivations (those for the behavior on the left and those away from the behavior on the right). Second, on the left side, which represents motivations toward the desired activity, labels are connected by arrows to the approach motivations (top arrow in box) and avoid motivations (bottom

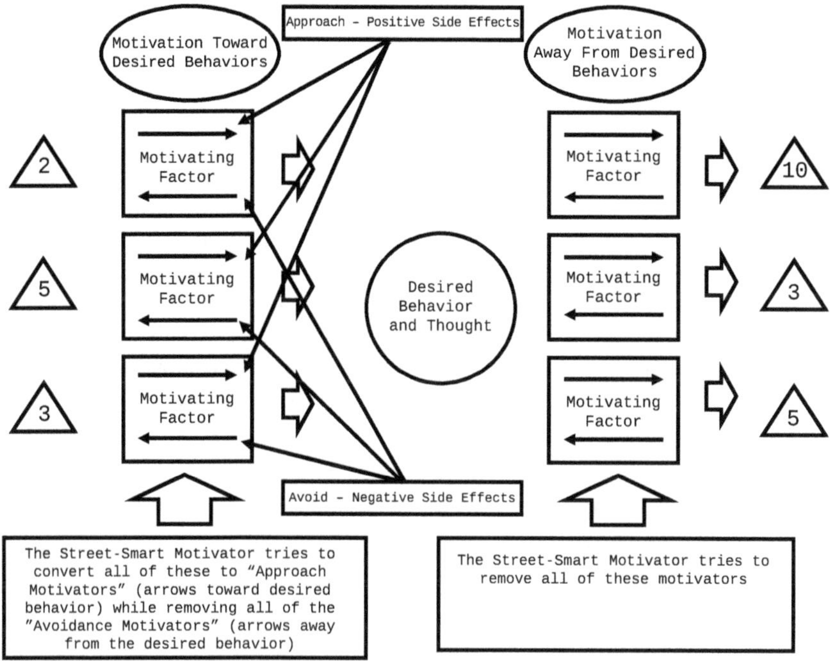

Figure 2.2 Weights Attached.

arrow in box). Remember that approach and avoid motivations on the left both represent motivations to do the thing you want them to do, but for very different reasons.

The weights attached to the motivations are made up and represent a scale of 1–10, with 10 being the most powerful. A quick look would show that in this case, the total motivational power on the left side to do the thing you are wanting the employee to learn/do is 10, while the total motivational power on the right side to not learn/do the thing you want them to do is 18. In this scenario, the employee will likely not learn/do the thing that you want them to do because they are more motivated to not do it.

This is where the power of demotivation really shows up. Whatever the 10 is on the right is a really big reason. Maybe that is the employee thinking that if they go down the road you are asking, they will eventually be out of a job (that's pretty big!). What normally happens here is that the leader and instructor try adding some motivation on the left side, not even thinking to remove motivations on the other side. The problem with that is that most of the motivations we add are low-level motivations, say ones and twos. Putting candy out for employees, or maybe some coffee and fruit, snazzing up our slide presentation, or adding a fun activity (which might actually not be).

It would take at least 6–8 such things to maybe come close to score on the other side. However, removing the false fear of working oneself out of a job (so long as it is false) would drop the score on the right side to 8 immediately. This sense of false fear, which are sadly quite common in the workplace, may take a few minutes to dispel, but it can be done and that will tilt the situation strongly and quickly in the right motivational direction. Now adding candy on the tables might really make a difference.

And, working the entire field would mean that you can have all of the motivation on the left side along with all positive long-term side effects for the individual and organization, or you can have a mixed bag, with some or even all of the motivations being avoidance motivations. In that case, you will get it done but not optimally and not expertly.

Motivational Field vs. Motivational Factors

In order to motivate Mike to wear his hardhat, and to also motivate him in a way that is efficient in the short and long term, and in a way that has significant, positive contextual benefits, the street-smart motivator will work with Mike to change the *motivational field*, and not simply focus on one or more motivational factors. There was a key there that shouldn't be missed. If you are ever hoping to become proficient at working with motivational fields rather than just factors, you are going to have to collaborate with those being led and those being taught. It simply can't be done to someone; it must be done *with* someone.

Notes

1 Taylor, J. E. (2021). *Motivational immediacy: Fostering engagement in adult learners.* Stylus.

2 Taylor, J. E. (2022). *Motivational immediacy in the workplace: Facilitating learner engagement in training environments.* Routledge.

3 Illeris, K. (2017). *How we learn: Learning and non-learning in school and beyond* (2nd ed.). Routledge.

4 Lewin, K. (2013). *A dynamic theory of personality – Selected papers.* Read Books, Ltd. (Original work published in 1935.)

5 Reeve, J. (2015). *Understanding motivation and emotion.* John Wiley & Sons.

6 Illeris, K. (2017). *How we learn: Learning and non-learning in school and beyond* (2nd ed.). Routledge

7 Schunk, D. E., & Zimmerman, B. J. (2007). Competence and control beliefs: Distinguishing the means and ends. In P. A. Alexander & P. H. Winne (Eds.), *Handbook of educational psychology* (2nd ed., pp. 349–367). Lawrence Erlbaum Associates.

8 Schunk, D. E., & Zimmerman, B. J. (2007). Competence and control beliefs: Distinguishing the means and ends. In P. A. Alexander & P. H. Winne (Eds.), *Handbook of educational psychology* (2nd ed., pp. 349–367). Lawrence Erlbaum Associates.

9 Elliot, A. J. (1999). Approach and avoidance motivation and achievement goals. *Educational Psychologist, 34*(3), 169–189.

10 Ferris, D. L., Johnson, R. E., Rosen, C. C., Djurdjevic, E., Chang, C. H., & Tan, J. A. (2012). When is success not satisfying? Integrating regulatory focus and approach/avoidance motivation theories to explain the relation between core self-evaluation and job satisfaction. *Journal of Applied Psychology, 98*(2), 342–353. https://doi.org/10.1037/a0029776

11 Nikitin, J., & Freund, A. M. (2015). What you want to avoid is what you see: Social avoidance motivation affects the interpretation of emotional faces. *Motivation and Emotion, 39*(3), 384–391. https://doi.org.10.1007/s11031-014-9459-5

12 Dijk, D. V., Seger-Guttmann, T., & Heller, D. (2013). Life-threatening event reduces subjective will-being through activating avoidance motivation: A longitudinal study. *Emotion, 13*(2), 216–225.

13 Nikitin, J., & Freund, A. M. (2015). What you want to avoid is what you see: Social avoidance motivation affects the interpretation of emotional faces. *Motivation and Emotion, 39*(3), 384–391. https://doi.org.10.1007/s11031-014-9459-5

14 Dijk, D. V., Seger-Guttmann, T., & Heller, D. (2013). Life-threatening event reduces subjective will-being through activating avoidance motivation: A longitudinal study. *Emotion, 13*(2), 216–225.

Chapter 3

Motivated to NOT Learn

If a street-smart motivator works with the learner's motivational field to foster the right kind of motivation for the right kind of things, one of the fundamental tasks of the street-smart motivator is to understand just what motivates people in the area of learning. With the world full of motivational literature, speeches, videos, and posters, one might think that things that motivate learners are common sense and intuitively obvious at this point. This likely would be true except for the fact that the motivational world we have been exposed to has, as I have noted in previous chapters, emphasized easy to remember misunderstandings instead of hard-earned clarity, and simple misconception over complicated reality.

To be specific, in the case of understanding what motivates learners, common practice has us focused only on what motivates learners to learn something and ignores just what motivates learners to *not* learn something. This has happened because of the incorrect idea that learners are motivated to learn or not motivated to learn, rather than assuming that learners can be motivated to learn or motivated to not learn (not the same thing as not being motivated to learn).

This incorrect understanding of human learning motivation has probably come about for many different reasons, but one of them is that we have tried to remain "positive" with learning. We all remember being in a "learn this or else" situation and typically don't wish it on anyone. But in our effort to be positive about learning, we have slipped into a misinformed teaching practice in which we think that all we need to be concerned about is what motivates our learners to want to learn what we want them to learn, rather than to think of all the many (some very good) reasons why they may more specifically be motivated to not learn.

Since not being motivated to learn is so often confused with being very motivated to *not* learn, consider a time when you were sitting comfortably at home reading a book or watching a movie. At some point, you may have noticed that you were a little thirsty and considered going to the kitchen to

DOI: 10.4324/9781003482079-4

get a glass of water. While slightly tempted to do it, you may have ended up staying where you were for a while longer because you were (a) very comfortably settled into the couch on a cold evening, and (b) deeply enjoying the thing you were reading or watching, which was at that moment at a pivotal point in the story. This, we might say, is a situation in which you are not motivated to get up and go get a glass of water. Similarly, one may simply not feel like mustering the energy to learn in a given moment. This would be someone who is not motivated to learn.

On the other hand, consider a situation in which you might be traveling in a distant place to which your body is not at all accustomed. You are feeling thirsty and there is a sink and a glass of water nearby. You look at it and shudder as you remember your first time drinking the local water while traveling to a distant place and the horrendous stomach trauma that followed. You may be thirsty, but you will *not* be touching that water under any circumstances unless you are a hair's breadth away from perishing of thirst. You are motivated to *not* drink that water.

Not being motivated to drink the water in the first scenario above is a lazy thought, but being motivated to not drink the water in the second scenario is an overbearing, almost militant thought. It is a hill to (almost) die on.

That is learning motivation in its essence. Being motivated to learn something can be powerful. Not being motivated to learn something may be a somewhat lazy thought, easily changed. Being motivated to not learn something is a hill to die on.

The previous chapter addressed a form of street-smart motivation that is savvy to the real-world conditions of leading and learning. Taking this into account, the action-oriented practitioner will as a next step dig in and search for all the prominent reasons (and maybe even some distant possibilities for good measure) that people are motivated to not learn. Because people are motivated to *not* learn, as often (and perhaps more) than they are motivated to learn, it is inefficient at best and ineffective at worst, to not spend some time thinking about why adults may be motivated to *not* do what you are wanting them to do or learn what you are wanting them to learn.

Going back to the figure from Chapter 2, shown again here as Figure 3.1, this chapter is focused on the motivational boxes on the right of the desired behavior. The boxes on the right represent motivational factors that drive a learner *away* from the desired thinking and behavior.

There are four significant points to be made in this chapter, the first of which was just stated:

- Engaging in a learning situation and refusing to engage in a learning situation are *both* motivated behaviors.
- There are four broad types of learning resistance.

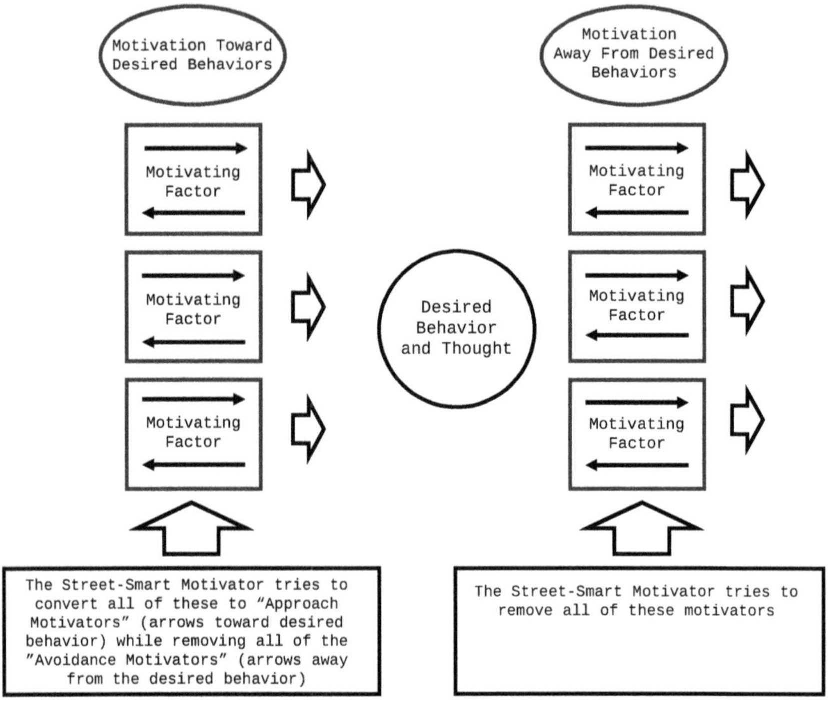

Figure 3.1 The Motivation Field.

- Emotion is key in learning motivation.
- Learning is about the *acceptance* of content, not merely the acquisition of content.

A theme in this book so far is that what we call things – that is, the words we use – and how we define them, matters in our pursuit of more and more effective leading, mentoring, and teaching. This chapter, as much as and perhaps more than the others, introduces a number of terms that are being used in very specific ways. Learning engagement and learning resistance are the most frequently used and frame out the concepts I am introducing.

Learning Engagement

Learning engagement has been viewed many different ways. Some have tended toward clumping engagement loosely with motivation. Again though, this is a shortcut that doesn't serve the expert professional well. Being sloppy never serves the expert well. Motivation and engagement are related, of course, but one is the thing we do (engagement), and the other is the reason we do it (motivation).

Engagement is "how invested people are in a given task, their conscientiousness and willingness to exert effort in order to master challenging content and difficult skills."[1] With regard to learning, it is "a psychological process, specifically, the attention, interest, investment, and effort students expend in the work of learning."[2] Learning requires a degree of willingness to mobilize the necessary energies (i.e., physical, emotional, and psychological), and learners who are willing to commit to this in any given learning context can be said to be engaged.

Learning Resistance

Motivation to *not* learn is often referred to as a "lack of motivation." Chapter 2 addressed just how incorrect this particular popular notion is and, more importantly, how much it can reduce our ability to be effective and efficient with people under our leadership or influence at work. The other very common term is learning resistance, but because of its history, learning resistance is a term that can only be used effectively after pains are taken to clearly specify the meaning that is intended. The adage about words having usage rather than definitions is particularly apt here. Many have used the term to refer to a learner who simply disagrees with something being taught or questions the reasoning of the one teaching. This is problematic, however, for any true leader or teacher because as the other old saying goes, "he who is convinced against his will is of the same opinion still." It would be difficult to find a very strong leader who thought the best way to influence people was to simply have them pretend to agree. Therefore, often the best long-term learners are those who ask the toughest questions up front. Authentic challenges to content lead to authentic learning of content over time.

The way I define it, *learning resistance is simply a lack of engagement on the part of the learner.*[3,4,5] It is a lack of openness to learning in a given situation. However, it is very often, though not always, highly motivated behavior. When situated in contrast to engagement, it can be generally viewed as a negative phenomenon. To be engaged *doesn't* mean that the learner gullibly accepts any given thing they hear, blindly adopts new ways of seeing things, or allows themselves to be manipulated by the teacher in ways that diminish their own individuality and agency. That sort of learning doesn't typically pan out all that well in the long-run for any organization within which it is the standard. Authentic learning is typically more resilient over time, as is almost anything that is authentic compared to anything that is fake or superficial. Engagement does mean, however, that the learner is present in the learning activity and mobilizes the emotional, psychological, cognitive, and physical energy and resources needed to try to learn something from the situation. And, of course, mobilizing the emotional, psychological, cognitive, and physical energy and resources needed to learn something requires lots of motivation. Learners who are truly engaged to learn in a given situation are always motivated individuals because engagement costs too high a price to provide for no perceived return.

Academics have spent a great deal of time arguing over the relationship between a number of different related terms such as motivation, engagement, and resistance. In this book, these terms are used in the following ways. Motivation is the underlying drive, typically psychological, that underlies a person's active engagement to learn something in some setting or to disengage from a learning situation. Engagement refers to the "psychological process, specifically, the attention, interest, investment, and effort [learners] expend in the work of learning."[6] It includes both cognitive investment[7] and psychic energy,[8] and it implies a learner's openness to learning in a given context.[9]

Resistance Is a Failure to Engage

Learning resistance can be defined as a state in which a learner is not open to learning in a specific learning situation as demonstrated through either active rejection or passive disengagement.[10,11,12] Defined this way, resistance has, as its more positive opposite, ***engagement***. Learning engagement, or rather, engagement with the learning ***situation*** (though not necessarily acceptance of the learning content) is considered a psychological process, specifically the attention, interest, investment, and effort students expend in the work of learning (Figure 3.2).[13]

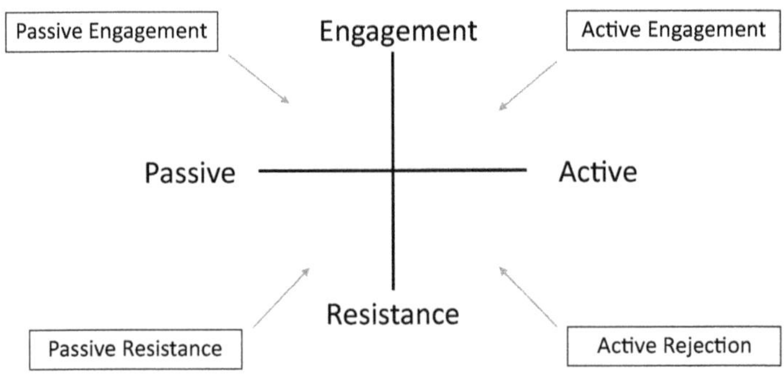

Figure 3.2 Learning Engagement-Resistance Continuum.

Source: Reprinted with Permission. Taylor (2014).

1. **Passive Engagement** – The learner is not resistant to the class or the content but is not actively mobilizing energy for learning in the learning context.
2. **Active Engagement** – The learner is purposefully mobilizing energy toward learning in the learning context.
3. **Passive Disengagement** – The learner is purposefully resisting and emotionally/psychologically closed to the learning activity (course or content), but is not actively mobilizing energy toward that resistance in the learning context.
4. **Active Rejection** – The learner is purposefully mobilizing energy for resistance in the learning context. Resistant behaviors and cognitions are present, and behaviors are typically overt.

A Note about Behavior vs. Cause

It is really important that the leader and teacher recognize that behavior is not, itself, learning resistance. Remembering that resistance as I am defining it here, refers to a lack of engagement, one has to learn to see through the manifested behavior and see the underlying cause of that behavior. An easy example that we may all be able to relate to is doodling in a classroom when listening to someone provide a lesson or lecture or speech on something. You may be able to relate to an experience when you were actually listening and engaged, but during which you continued to draw on the edge of your notepad or handout. Perhaps you were continually tracing over a letter until you nearly wore a hole in the paper, or maybe if you are more gifted, you were converting some mark on the page into a likeness of a famous work of art.

You may, however, also be able to think of a time when you were nearly bored out of your mind and were doodling on a page to maintain your sanity as you sat there. In this latter example, you were not engaged at all and rather than your drawing being an idle energy outlet while listening and thinking, it was a lifeline alternative to engagement with the unpleasant experience.

Certainly, more complicated examples could be drawn on, but in nearly all cases any given behavior could indicate that you are actually very engaged with the learning situation or very withdrawn from it. Arguing with the instructor is another example. Arguing could be a sign of disrespect, disruption, and disengagement. But it often is instead a sign of passion, intensity, and high-level engagement with the learning situation. It is for these reasons that one should be more concerned with what is going on in the learner's mind, that with the learner's behavior in a given context. The behavior is certainly a starting place, but it cannot be the ending place.

Four Types of Learning Resistance

Learning resistance can be seen many different ways, but all forms of it can be organized into roughly four different groups. It will immediately become obvious that there is some overlap between the categories. As with all organizing structures, they are helpful in understanding a range of ideas, but are not intended to reflect an unrealistic rigidity. I have clustered them according to the underlying reasons for the behavior, not the specific behavior itself. This is important and necessary because the same exact external behavior could be an indication of resistance or engagement (arguing with the instructor, for instance).

The following four types of resistance – Environmental, Epistemological, Psychological, and Sociocultural[14,15] – are described below in the order of what are typically the simplest to the most difficult to mitigate in the workplace.

Environmental Resistance (I Can't Hear over That Drilling)

Environmental resistance is what it sounds like. It is a motivation to not learn, on the part of the learner, due to some environmental condition or distraction. Importantly, environmental resistance refers only to those aspects of the environment that are in close proximity of the specific learning situation. Examples of this are noise pollution (e.g., loud construction work), poorly controlled temperatures such as hot stuffy rooms, or cold, damp rooms, significantly bland or low-quality presentations (or bad leadership), and other such factors local to the learning situation. Although typically environmental resistance has to do with things connected directly to the learning space itself, the immediate effects of outside factors, such as a fight with a family member on the way to work, could be included. Other, more long-term and complex family problems would fit in the other categories below.

One positive aspect of environmental is that it is often both easier to recognize and also to fix. This, of course, is not always the case, but often it is a simple matter of adjusting the temperature, closing a door, moving a training location, or having the conversation in a different office. In cases in which the employee–learner is upset from a recent outside interaction, being provided a few minutes to get themselves together is typically worth the few minutes it may take. It is important to note here that sometimes, for resistance in any of these categories, there is no way to completely fix it in a given context. That does not, however, alter the fact that it always makes sense to try, since often it can be improved.

Epistemological Resistance (What Are We Doing Here?)

Epistemology concerns the concept of truth – how we see it, what we think it is, and how we evaluate it as truth to begin with. Epistemological resistance refers to learning resistance caused by a disconnect or mismatch between the learner's and teacher's conception or understanding of (a) what learning is and/or (b) what criteria should be used to evaluate truth claims.

Epistemological resistance can be seen in cases in which the employees are using quite different criteria for evaluating truth claims than their employers and, by extension, their instructors and trainers.[16] If, for example, an individual believes that learning is about obtaining a physical skill, the ability to do something, and that individual is placed in a leadership class in which they are subjected to a lengthy instructional sequence on some form of leadership competency, the mismatch between the understanding of knowledge between the employee and employer could have significantly negative effects in terms of training efficacy.

If an employee thinks you are sharing with them how to do a specific task, but you are actually taking time to invest in them in an effort to help them develop broadly into a different type of employee altogether (i.e., future manager), the entire event can be viewed by the employee as a convoluted mess and therefore, reasonably, a waste of time. Conversely, if an employee thinks you are trying to school them in the family business, but you are simply trying to teach them how to use a specific piece of equipment, their assessment criteria will not match your educative methods. There will not be a goodness of fit between their expectations and your own.

Another routine dynamic is where a leader tries to instruct an employee or colleague in some form but teaches them something that does not match up at all to the real-world (real-work) environment in which the application is supposed to be employed. To illuminate this more clearly, here are a few real examples from my own work with consulting and conducting research studies:

- School teachers forced to sit through a 4-hour in-service course on how to use tablets in the classroom when they had no technology in their school.
- Parcel service employees who were subjected to a course on unsafe and prohibited behaviors over half of which were (a) required in order to actually do the job, and/or (b) something they were specifically told to do by supervisors on the shop floor.
- Law enforcement officers taught to use a particular criminal charge that was not valid in their jurisdiction.

- Electricians verbally taught to demonstrate something to other learners in a way that was entirely unsafe for the learner (okay, that one might have been me).

The fact is, workplace leading and training is shot through with this sort of thing, and learners are smart enough to ignore it when they hear it. There are some very complex but effective ways to handle this, and they will be shared in depth in later chapters, but there are also some very simple ways to mitigate this type of resistance. First and foremost, do your homework and don't teach faulty stuff. That is easier to say than do sometimes, but there are other ways also. For instance, in the final example above, when the learners pointed out that my particular idea would, in fact, be harmful – and I think the direct quote was "would kill everyone two times a day" – I was able to respond first with "how so?" and then with "so what then do *you* think can be done to apply this learning principle?" This approach is not optimal, since it begins with a bad teaching statement, but it is better than letting it lie. Learners may not have the knowledge we wish to give them, but they are not generally foolish any more than we are, nor do they wish to have their time wasted, any more than we do. The above sorts of teaching and leading behaviors will most often motivate learners to not learn what we are teaching and not follow where we are leading.

Psychological Resistance (Oh No! I Have Been Here Before)

Psychological resistance is characterized by largely internal factors. Cognitive and/or psychological resistance is related to issues of self-efficacy,[17,18] learned helplessness,[19] disinterest/boredom,[20,21,22] identity,[23,24,25] and overconfidence or presumption.[26,27]

One particularly interesting psychological factor of resistance has to do with personal identity. Knud Illeris identifies the connection between one's identity and one's work responsibilities and skills.[28] This is noteworthy because individuals are naturally very protective when they feel that their individual identity is being threatened. In the workplace, we may think we are simply telling an employee with 20 years of experience to switch from paper records to computer records (what's the big deal?) while they are hearing that we want them to change who they actually believe they are. This is another area where thinking like a leader rather than an instructor will be helpful. Being sensitive to how people attach themselves to various skills, practices, and jobs is vital for fostering needed change in others.

Sociocultural Resistance (This Entire Thing Is Unfair)

Sociocultural resistance – to borrow a term popularly attributed to Vygotskian[29] ideas – refers to learning resistance that has as its source, social or cultural dynamics. Contemporary society has focused a good bit of attention to issues such as justice and equity in the workplace and it is not surprising that there is a great deal of disagreement with just how much time, energy, and money should be spent on investing in social justice in the workplace. Wherever one comes down on the issue, and politics aside, the expert motivator cannot afford to ignore anything that is a part of the motivational field of those in the sphere of influence. Teaching and leading are about the other person and if the other person feels marginalized, disrespected, and cheated, you will not teach them much or lead them far.

With regards to all four types of learning resistance discussed here, a full academic treatment of the scholarship behind this information is available in two academic books on this topic, but a brief list of the causes that can be found in the academic literature is shown in Table 3.1.

Table 3.1 Suggested Causes of Learning Resistance

Causes of Learning Resistance
Resistance to dominant culture[30,31,32,33,34,35,36]
Conflict between old and new learning[37]
Discomfort due to accommodative learning[38,39] (transformative/conceptual change)
Cultural mismatch[40,41,42]
Immersion in the learning experience[43]
Disliking courses, administration, and/or educational system/school environment/initiatives[44,45,46,47,48]
Lack of interest, disinterest, and boredom[49,50,51]
Low self-esteem; fear of the unknown/anxiety; dislike of the teacher; irrelevancy of the material; inappropriate level of required learning[52,53,54,55,56]
Development of the personal will; differentiation from others; successful development of personal identity; role confusion[57,58,59,60,61,62]
Examination culture in school; mismatch of teacher and learner goals[63]
Mismatch between learner's life experience and formal education[64,65]
Resistance to change study methods and habits[66,67]
Failure to "buy in" to learning objectives[68]
Teacher immediacy[69,70]
Brand loyalty – "Tribal Affiliation" and "Hero Worship"[71]
Family Issues and other external factors[72,73]
Dislike of the Teacher[74]

Range and Intensity of Learning Resistance

Because learners can be motivated to not learn for so many different reasons, it is difficult to identify where it most often exists, and in what intensity. However, as a general rule of thumb, it makes sense that when the learning subject requires more emotional disruption, there will likely be more resistance to engagement. An adaptation from Gold's[75] work on this is shown in Figure 3.3.

In the diagram, the type of learning fostered in a given situation ranges from simple rote memorization on the bottom, to highly complex conceptual change and transformation on the top. The state of the learner is depicted on the other axis, with low emotional disruption on the left, and high emotional disruption on the right. Since resistance is such a complex interaction of internal and external factors, it is impossible to characterize to a high degree, much less predict, a given level of learning resistance, but as a general rule, one would expect that more complex forms of learning, such as conceptual change, and more emotional disruption in the learner would both result in a greater degree of learning resistance.

The reason I have put these on two dimensions rather than one is to allow for a learning situation that might be simple and non-threatening, but to which the learner comes in a state of incidental emotional disruption. For instance, an employee might arrive at a safety briefing after having had a very bad morning that started with a domestic argument and ended with not being able to find a parking space. In this case, the emotional disruption

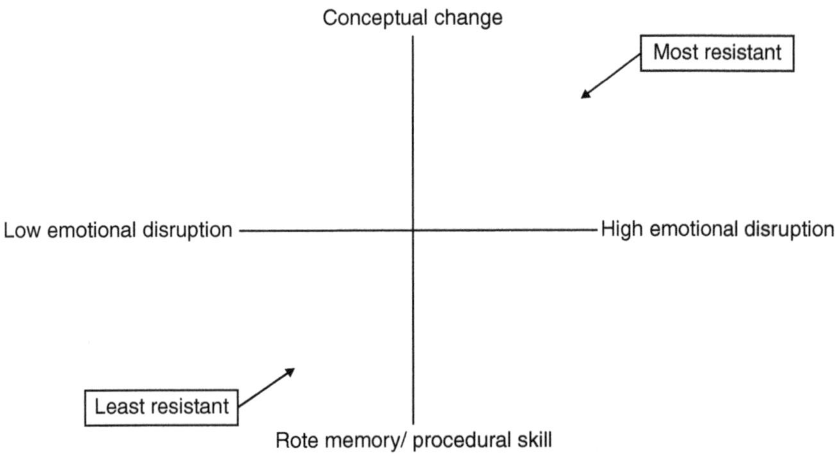

Figure 3.3 Range and Strength of Learning Resistance.

Source: Adapted from Gold (2005).

is high, and even if the learning is simple, i.e., rote memorization of facts, it is likely the learner will be resistant.

Likewise, in cases of very complex and normally stressful forms of learning, such as conceptual change – "we are taking this unit in an entirely different direction..." – certain learners may be in a good place in their personal lives and/or have a personality that is conducive to handling such tasks. This situation would represent an intersection of situational and dispositional factors but could result in stressful learning that does not disrupt the emotions of the learner to a significant degree.

Those exceptions given, as a general rule more complex forms of learning such as conceptual change and transformational change typically result in the learner experiencing more emotional stress, anxiety, and disruption, and because of this, as learning shifts upward from simple to complex learning, more learners would tend to experience a greater degree of naturally occurring emotional disruption, shifting into the upper right quadrant.

Finally, looking at the diagram as a whole, the strongest resistance behaviors and cognitions would indicate in the upper right quadrant, and the bottom left quadrant would represent the area with the least or weakest resistance.

Motivation, Emotion, and Acceptance

Going back to the original three points listed at the beginning of this chapter, here are the key takeaways from the information provided here:

Engaging in a learning situation and refusing to engage in a learning situation are both motivated behaviors. Because the most effective motivators are able to work within the full motivational field of the learner, rather than a few individual motivational factors, it is vital that it is understood that a range of motivational factors lead learners to learn something and to avoid it. Beyond this, even those motivations that drive a learner to learn something may result in the learner learning the thing in order to gain something (approach motivation) or to avoid something (avoidance motivation). The former is generally healthy and efficient, while the latter is generally unhealthy and inefficient, at least in the long-run. In order to be the most effective and efficient as a motivator (i.e., leader, mentor, and instructor), seeing the proper connection between motivation and learning is required.

Emotion is key in learning motivation.[76,77,78] Although I am making the case in this book that leading is teaching and vice versa, the classical distinction between the two has left most leaders understanding that emotion is key in leading anyone anywhere, while educators have learned to "go it alone" and disregard emotion as an unnecessary complication to simply "learning something."

Taking all of this complexity together a quite simple truth emerges for the one who would lead, mentor, and teach – learning is not about learners simply acquiring content, it is about learners accepting content as good. It is about learners agreeing and believing that a thing ought to be done. Teaching, therefore, is about fostering acceptance and buy-in from the learner, just like leading is about casting a shared vision and fostering a collaborative drive toward it.

Notes

1 Renniger, K. A., Yanyon, R., & Kern, H. M. (2018). Motivation, engagement, and interest: "In the end, it came down to you and how you think of the problem." In F. Fischer, C. Hmelo-Silver, S. R. Goldman, & P. Reimann (Eds.), *International handbook of the learning sciences* (p. 119). Routledge.
2 Marks, H. M. (2000). Student engagement in instructional activity: Patterns in the elementary, middle, and high school years [pp. 154–155]. *American Educational Research Journal, 37*(1), 153–184.
3 Taylor, J. E. (2022). *Motivational immediacy: Fostering engagement in adult learners.* Stylus.
4 Taylor, J. E. (2022). *Motivational immediacy in the workplace: Facilitating learner engagement in training environments.* Routledge.
5 Taylor, J. E. (2014). Starting with the learner: Designing learner engagement into the curriculum. In V. C. X. Wang & V. C. Bryan (Eds.), *Andragogical and pedagogical methods for curriculum and program development* (pp. 55–80). IGI Global. https://doi.org/10.4018/978-1-4666-5872-1.ch004
6 Marks, H. M. (2000). Student engagement in instructional activity: Patterns in the elementary, middle, and high school years [pp. 154–155]. *American Educational Research Journal, 37*(1), 153–184.
7 Fredricks, J. A., Blumenfeld, P. C., & Paris, A. H. (2004). School engagement: Potential of the concept, state of the evidence. *Review of Educational Research, 74*(1), 59–109.
8 Csikszentmihalyi, M. (1990). *Flow: The psychology of optimal experience.* Harper & Row Publishers.
Cutcher, L. (2009). Resisting change from within and without the organization. *Journal of Organizational Change Management, 22*(3), 275–289. https://doi.org/10.1108/09534810910951069
9 Taylor, J., & Lounsbury, J. W. (2016). Measuring learning resistance to workplace training. *International Journal of Adult Vocational Education and Technology, 7*(1), 25–38.
10 Taylor, J. E. (2022). *Motivational immediacy: Fostering engagement in adult learners.* Stylus.
11 Taylor, J. E. (2022). *Motivational immediacy in the workplace: Facilitating learner engagement in training environments.* New York.
12 Taylor, J. E. (2014). Starting with the learner: Designing learner engagement into the curriculum. In V. C. X. Wang & V. C. Bryan (Eds.), *Andragogical and pedagogical methods for curriculum and program development* (pp. 55–80). IGI Global. https://doi.org/10.4018/978-1-4666-5872-1.ch004
13 Marks, H. M. (2000). Student engagement in instructional activity: Patterns in the elementary, middle, and high school years [pp. 154–155]. *American Educational Research Journal, 37*(1), 153–184.

14 Taylor, J. E. (2022). *Motivational immediacy: Fostering engagement in adult learners.* Stylus.
15 Taylor, J. E. (2022). *Motivational immediacy in the workplace: Facilitating learner engagement in training environments.* Routledge.
16 Salaman, G., & Butler, J. (1990). Why managers won't learn. *Management Education and Development, 21*, 183–191.
17 Bandura, A. (1986). *Social foundations of thought and action: A social cognitive theory.* Prentice-Hall.
18 Schunk, D. (1995). Self-efficacy and education and instruction. In J. D. Maddux (Ed.), *Self-efficacy, adaptation, and adjustment: Theory, research, and application* (pp. 281–303). Springer. https://doi.org/10.1007/978-1-4419-6868-5
19 Maier, S. F., & Seligman, M. E. (1976). Learned helplessness: Theory and evidence. *Journal of Experimental Psychology: General, 105*(1), 3–46.
20 Schraw, G., Flowerday, T., & Lehman, S. (2001). Increasing situational interest in the classroom. *Educational Psychology Review, 13*(3), 211–224.
21 Schraw, G., & Lehman, S. (2001). Situational interest: A review of the literature and directions for future research. *Educational Psychology Review, 13*(1), 23–52.
22 Shaw, S. M., Caldwell, L. L., & Kleiber, D. A. (1996). Boredom, stress, and social control in daily activities of adolescents. *Journal of Leisure Research, 28*(4), 274–292.
23 Illeris, K. (2007). *How we learn: Learning and non-learning in school and beyond.* Routledge.
24 Illeris, K. (2011). *The fundamentals of workplace learning: Understanding how people learn in working life.* Routledge.
25 Torrance, P. (1949). The phenomenon of resistance in learning. *Journal of Abnormal and Social Psychology, 45*(4), 592–597.
26 Taylor, J. E. (2010). *Resistance to learning in mandatory training contexts: A psychometric approach to measuring resistance and related factors.* [Unpublished doctoral dissertation]. University of Tennessee.
27 Jarvis, P. (1992). *Paradoxes of learning: On becoming an individual in society.* Jossey-Bass.
28 Illeris, K. (2011). *The fundamentals of workplace learning: Understanding how people learn in working life.* Routledge.
29 Vygotsky, L. S. (1978). *Mind in society: The development of higher psychological processes.* Harvard University Press.
30 Giroux, H. A. (1983). *Theory and resistance in education: A pedagogy for the opposition.* South Bergin & Garvey Publishers, Inc.
31 Moore, H. A. (2007). Student resistance in sociology classrooms: Tools for learning and teaching. *Sociological Viewpoints, 23*, 29–44.
32 Ogbu, J. (1991). Cultural diversity and school experience. In C. E. Walsh (Ed.), *Literacy as praxis: Culture, language, and pedagogy* (pp. 25–50). Ablex.
33 McNamee, K., Atwood, K., Noddings, N., & Taylor, P. C. (2002). Power. In J. Wallace, & W. Louden (Eds.), *Dilemmas of science teaching* (pp. 98–111). Routledge.
34 Jarvensivu, A., & Koski, P. (2012). Combating learning. *Journal of Workplace Learning, 24*(1), 5–18. https://doi.org/10.1108/13665621211191078
35 Hughes, J. (2005). Bringing emotion to work: Emotional intelligence, employee resistance and the reinvention of character. *Work, Employment and Society, 19*(3), 603–625. https://doi.org/10.1177/0950017005055675
36 Atherton, J. (1999). Resistance to learning: A discussion based on participants in in-service professional training programmes. *Journal of Vocational Education and Training, 51*(1), 77–90.

37 Salaman, G., & Butler, J. (1990). Why managers won't learn. *Management Education and Development*, *21*, 183–191.
38 Brady, T. C. (1975). *A study in the application of the C. A. Curran Counseling-Learning Model to adults.* [Unpublished doctoral dissertation]. Walden University.
39 Cohen, J. (2018). Overcoming SMEs' resistance to learning through a metaphor/storyline approach: A qualitative assessment of a novel marketing intervention. *Middle East Journal of Business*, *13*(1), 17–31.
40 Seiler, G., Tobin, K., & Sokolic, J. (2001). Design, technology, and science: Sites for learning, resistance, and social reproduction in urban schools. *Journal of Research in Science Teaching*, *38*(7), 746–767.
41 Cutcher, L. (2009). Resisting change from within and without the organization. *Journal of Organizational Change Management*, *22*(3), 275–289. https://doi.org/10.1108/09534810910951069
42 Moscovici, H. (2003). The way I see it: Resisting teacher control or canceling the effect of science immersion. *Journal of Research in Science Teaching*, *40*(1), 98–100.
43 Quigley, B. A. (1997). *Rethinking literacy education: The critical need for practice-based change.* Jossey-Bass.
44 Atherton, J. (1999). Resistance to learning: A discussion based on participants in in-service professional training programmes. *Journal of Vocational Education and Training*, *51*(1), 77–90.
45 Hultman, K. (1995). Training 101: Scaling the wall of resistance. *Training & Development*, *49*(10), 15–18.
46 Garber, S. H. (2002, April 1–5). *"Hearing their voices": Perceptions of high-school students who evidence resistance to schooling* [Paper presentation]. Annual Meeting of the American Educational Research Association, New Orleans, LA, United States.
47 Baker, E. W., & Hill, S. (2017). Investigating student resistance and student perceptions of course quality and instructor performance in a flipped information systems classroom. *Information Systems Educational Journal*, *15*(6), 17–26.
48 Sun, A. (1995). Development and factor analyses of the student resistance to schooling inventory. *Educational and Psychological Measurement*, *55*(5), 841–849.
49 Kruglanski, A. W., Fishback, A., Woolley, K., Belanger, J. J., Chernikova, M., Molinario, E., & Pierro, A. (2018). A structural model of intrinsic motivation: On the psychology of means-ends fusion. *Psychological Review*, *125*(2), 165–182. https://doi.org/10.1037/rev0000095
50 Quigley, B. A. (1997). *Rethinking literacy education: The critical need for practice-based change.* Jossey-Bass.
51 Brookfield, S. D. (2006). *The skillful teacher: On technique, trust, and responsiveness in the classroom* (2nd ed.). Jossey-Bass.
52 Reyes, M. E. (Ed.). (2002). *Proceedings of the Annual Meeting of the National Association of African American Studies, the National Association of Hispanic and Latino Studies, the National Association of Native American Studies, and the International Association of Asian Studies.* https://eric.ed.gov/?id=ED477416
53 Quigley, B. A. (1997). *Rethinking literacy education: The critical need for practice-based change.* Jossey-Bass
54 Kunst, M. S. (1959). Learning disabilities: Their dynamics. *Social Worker*, *4*(1), 95–101.

55 Smith, I. (2005). Continuing professional development and workplace learning 13. *Library Management*, *26*(8/9), 519–522.
56 Caplin, M. D. (1969). Resistance to learning. *Peabody Journal of Education*, *47*(1), 36–39. learning outcomes. In S. Vosniadou (Ed.), *The handbook of research of conceptual change* (2nd ed., pp. 49–70). Routledge. https://doi.org/10.4324/9780203154472.ch3
57 Cutcher, L. (2009). Resisting change from within and without the organization. *Journal of Organizational Change Management*, *22*(3), 275–289. https://doi.org/10.1108/09534810910951069
58 Rank, O. (1945). *Will therapy and truth in reality*. Knopf.
59 Lecky, P. (1945). *Self-consistency; A theory of personality*. Island Press.
LeFebvre, L., & Allen, M. (2014). Teacher immediacy and student learning: An examination of lecture/laboratory and self-contained course sections. *Journal of the Scholarship of Teaching and Learning*, *14*(2), 29–45.
60 Kidd, J. R. (1959). *How adults learn: Tapping the great learning potential ... a synthesis of theory and experience exploring new knowledge for best teaching results*. Association Press.
61 Goisman, R. M. (1988). Resistances to learning behavior therapy. *American Journal of Psychotherapy*, *32*(1), 67–75.
62 Jing, H. (2006). Learning resistance in metacognition training? An exploration of mismatches between learner and teacher agendas. *Language Teaching Research*, *10*(1), 95–117.
63 Dembo, M. H., & Seli, H. P. (2004). Student's resistance to change in learning strategies courses. *Journal of Developmental Education*, *27*(3), 2–11.
64 Quigley, B. A. (1997). *Rethinking literacy education: The critical need for practice-based change*. Jossey-Bass.
65 Hultman, K. (1995). Training 101: Scaling the wall of resistance. *Training & Development*, *49*(10), 15–18.
66 White, J., Pinnegar, S., & Esplin, P. (2010). When learning and change collide: Examining student claims to have "learned nothing". *The Journal of General Education*, *59*(2), 125–140. https://doi.org/10.5325/jgeneeduc.59.2.0124
67 Illeris, K. (2003). Workplace learning and learning theory. *Journal of Workplace Learning*, *15*(4), 167–178. https://doi.org/10.1108/13665620310474615
68 Burroughs, N. F., Kearney, P., & Plax, T. G. (1989). Compliance-resistance in the college classroom. *Communication Education*, *38*(3), 214–229. https://doi.org/10.1080/03634528909378758
69 Burroughs, N. F. (2007). A reinvestigation of the relationship of teacher nonverbal immediacy and student compliance-resistance with learning. *Communication Education*, *56*(4), 453–475. https://doi.org.10.1080/03634520701530896
70 Gold, J. (2005). Anxiety, conflict, and the resistance in learning an integrative perspective on psychotherapy. *Journal of Psychotherapy Integration*, *15*(4), 374–383. https://doi.org/10.1037/1053-0479.15.4.374
71 Garber, S. H. (2002, April 1–5). *"Hearing their voices": Perceptions of high-school students who evidence resistance to schooling* [Paper presentation]. Annual Meeting of the American Educational Research Association, New Orleans, LA, United States.
72 Layte, R. (2017). Why do working-class kids do worse in school? An empirical test of two theories of educational disadvantage. *European Sociological Review*, *33*(4), 489–503. https://doi.org/10.1093/esr/jcx054

73 Illeris, K. (2017). *How we learn: Learning and non-learning in school and beyond* (2nd ed.). Routledge.
74 Garber, S. H. (2002, April 1–5). *"Hearing their voices": Perceptions of high-school students who evidence resistance to schooling* [Paper presentation]. Annual Meeting of the American Educational Research Association, New Orleans, LA, United States.
75 Gold, J. (2005). Anxiety, conflict, and the resistance in learning an integrative perspective on psychotherapy. *Journal of Psychotherapy Integration*, *15*(4), 374–383. https://doi.org/10.1037/1053-0479.15.4.374
76 Taylor, J. E. (2022). *Motivational immediacy: Fostering engagement in adult learners.* Stylus.
77 Taylor, J. E. (2022). *Motivational immediacy in the workplace: Facilitating learner engagement in training environments.* Routledge.
78 Giroux, H. A. (2001). *Theory and resistance in education.* Bergin & Garvey.

Chapter 4

Motivational Immediacy and Effectual Learning

It is at the juncture of *motivational immediacy* (MI) that the true power of aligning leading and teaching manifests itself. All of the concepts covered so far lead in a very specific direction and demand a number of clear implications for leading, teaching, and learning in the workplace.

A Quick Review

Motivation Is Bi-Directional

Motivation is a driving force that pushes an individual toward something *or away* from it. It is essential that motivation be viewed as the neutral dynamic that it is so that we can have a clear view of the motivational task before us – providing and enhancing some motivations and removing others. Motivation is a driving force. It is up to the expert leader to manage it so that it too works for the shared vision of the community in question. Leadership most definitely extends to the organization's motivational fields.

Fields Not Factors

Those who would be experts at working with people in leading, mentoring, and teaching, must reckon with the motivational fields in which those persons exist, rather than simply thinking of the traditionally tagged factors at play. For one thing, the actual factors change over time (i.e., being recognized at a work party may be less important to the contemporary employee than a flexible work schedule), and for another, motivational factors are just cogs in the wheels of the motivational system of which we are all embedded. The expert leader, mentor, and instructor must be able to work within the system and context of the learner to enhance the power of existing motivators toward the desired viewpoint or activity, remove motivators that drive

DOI: 10.4324/9781003482079-5

the learner away from the desired viewpoint or activity, and, beyond all of this, must work to change the valence for each of these positive motivators so that learners are motivated to achieve a desired end rather than to avoid an undesired one.

That one, rather long paragraph is an entire career's worth of hard work and skill development on the part of those who would be experts. It is an effort worth making and one of the many such commitments that mark out the few who rise above in the workplace.

Resistance Is Real (and for Good Reason)

Once one comes to terms with the fact that motivation is a neutral force that can drive a learner toward or away from any sort of learning that comes their way, it is a natural next step to acknowledge that there are many reasons that learners fail to engage in learning situations in the workplace. Some of the reasons are not very good ones, to be fair, but many of them make perfectly good sense if they are fairly considered. Either way, the expert doesn't have to agree with them, or even to sympathize with them (though sympathy can help sometimes). The expert does, however, need to empathize with the learner if any good teaching and leading is going to occur.

The most important take away from a study of learning resistance, though, is not the various factors that cause resistance, but the fact that learning is not at all, in the end, a simple matter of acquiring some content that is spoon fed in a classroom or around a water cooler. Although there is certainly acquisition of content involved in the process, the leader knows that it is mostly about the acceptance of content instead. One of the most significant training problems in the working world at the present time is that of minimal training transfer – employee–learners don't actually *do* any of the stuff that they indicate that they have learned in the workplace training room.

And, most of us can relate to this. Have you ever texted while driving (we know this is an unsafe practice)? Have you ever had one drink to many? One desert too many? Too much coffee? Gone to bed without brushing your teeth? These are all things about which we know better. Truly powerful workplace learning always involves buying in to the fact that one *ought* to do something and feels strongly enough about it that one typically *does* do that something, even when no one is looking. If you increase your ability to facilitate this sort of learning in the workplace, you will be among the very best leaders in the workplace domain. The key to doing so is to fully grasp the principles of motivational immediacy and to develop practical methods to live it on a daily basis.

Putting It All Together

Global vs. Local Motivation

I once had an instructor at a military leadership school say that he had it pretty easy because his learners were highly motivated. I asked him (of course) what he meant by that and he readily shared that each of those in the school had a strong drive to become a leader in the military branch they were in. Further discussion revealed that there were difficult topics and occasional bad days, despite their generally high levels of motivation, but that it was to be expected. This instructor was exactly right – it is to be expected. It is to be expected even among those who are highly motivated for some sort of long-term goal of which the present learning experience is only a part. Difficult topics and bad days are a routine part of the instructional world, and no kind of distant city on a hill can overcome it.

Real-life experience in the classroom is itself a great teacher, and no matter of empirical scholarship can replace it. For anyone who has taught in any sort of prolonged instructional program, you have experienced the rough topic and the difficult day. The fact of the matter is that being motivated for a long-term goal, something I refer to as global motivation,[1,2] is no match for trying to learn on a day that you overslept, had a terrible fight with your significant other, received bad medical news, or, perhaps most common, managed to get no sleep the night before. In these situations, there is just too much space between the learning task you are immediately faced with, and the long-term goal you are shooting for.

Global motivation is good, and it has power in learning situations. In fact, it likely has the best power to sustain a learner in the long-run – to stay at it. Its great failing, however, is in the here and now. This is a big problem because although there are certainly types of long-term learning that trickles in for a learner, almost all of our workplace training is in the here and now. Here and now motivation, or local motivation, is what drives a learner in any given moment to dig deep, marshal the resources, and lean into the learning experience. Whenever someone is really trying very hard to learn something in a given moment, there is almost always local motivation at play. Global motivation is a powerful tool in the toolbox, so to speak, but it has a great weakness that can severely limit its efficacy. The good news is that it can be addressed with a little effort.

Means-End-Fusion (MEF)

In 2018, as a part of a very long and, for most, tedious discussion about the nature of intrinsic and extrinsic motivation, a small group of scholars defined extrinsic motivation in a significantly different way that it has been largely conceived in the past.[3] The psychological milieu in which the information was embedded is (thankfully) outside the scope of this discussion, but the concepts are directly related and vital for the expert motivator.

Simply put, with every action, there is a desired end, and a required means. The desired end is the motivational drive, while the required means are what stand in the way. The more we desire the end, the more we are willing (and able) to remain focused and to achieve the tasks required to achieve the end we desire. Some means are in very close proximity to the ends. For instance, going into the kitchen and pouring water to drink is pretty close in proximity to drinking the water and quenching our thirst. Other means though are quite far removed from the ends they support. Consider putting money away in retirement for 30 years down the road. The difficulty of giving up things in the present so that there will be a payoff decades away is a much more difficult task because the ends are stretched out so far from the required means.

Ari Kruglanski and a group of others used a more academic sketch of this dynamic to differentiate extrinsic from intrinsic motivation.[4] The closer the means are to the end, the more intrinsic the motivation is, and the further the means are from the end the more extrinsic the motivation is. MEF is a related concept that refers to bridging the gap between the means and the ends for motivated behaviors to become strong, more sustained over time, and practically powerful.[5]

What matters here, for the topic at hand, is that global motivation, as I described it above, is almost always an end that is very far removed from the means that are required to obtain it. Despite this, it is the "go-to" leaders and trainers invoke more than any other to ensure that those in their sphere of influence are really engaging in the learning process. The takeaway for the expert motivator is that global motivation is *not* the bus to catch when trying to influence others in a powerful, sustained way. What is required is a consistent, pervasive effort on the part of the leader and instructor to facilitate MEF so that the learner is motivated in the present moment to engage with you on whatever topic is necessary for their growth or the growth of the organizational community at large.[6,7]

Remember, being motivated to have a certification in human resource development does not mean that one will be motivated to dig deep, on any given Tuesday morning at 8:30am (with terrible coffee) to engage on some 45-minute required module on federal employment statutes. It is, however, precisely these moments that the expert leader and trainer is called upon to foster motivation in each and every learner in that classroom. Are we up for the challenge?

Motivational Immediacy

MI is the culmination of all of these realities and can be seen as a *state* of being in a moment-by-moment motivational relationship with the student. Defined as an *action process*, MI is the practice of purposefully adopting as a part of one's instructional method, the consistent, pervasive, and habitual attempt to connect with each individual learner and ensure that the learner is motivated in the immediate sense, regardless of whether global motivation is present or not.

The concept of immediacy may date back as far as the work of Danish philosopher Soren Kirkegaard,[8] but in its present form is largely thought to have originated with Albert Mehrabian's communication theory and focused on verbal and non-verbal immediacy, which emphasized the perception of closeness one feels to the communicator.[9] The concept was carried over into the education world with a related and more specific idea of *teacher immediacy*.[10] More immediacy results in better communication and better (and more) learning, and it was a natural progression to apply the term to the instructor's motivational relationship with the learner.[11]

Since developing this idea a few years back and writing about it in a couple of other books,[12,13] it has become obvious that the outer edges of MI extend much further than the above definition permits. Figure 4.1 shows the full, expanded concept of MI and how it is a part of a much broader and holistic dynamic.

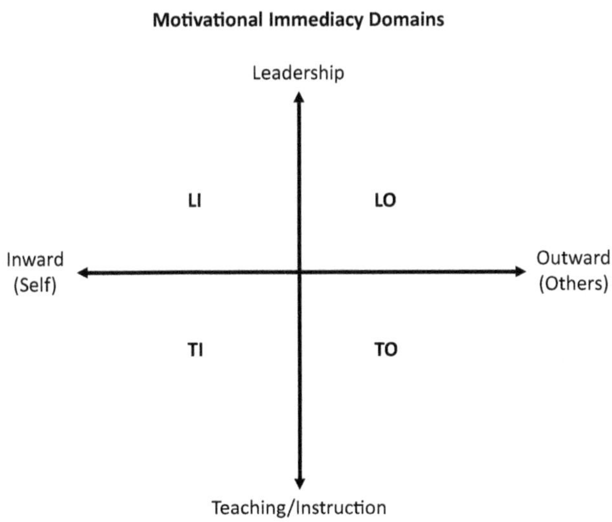

Figure 4.1 Motivational Immediacy Domains.

In Figure 4.1, the vertical axis shows the span from teaching and instruction specifically (at the lower end) to leadership at the top end. It is likely true that MI could be extended into many other domains, but leading and teaching are so very tightly connected that it made sense to make them the endpoints. While there is always an overlap between the two, in a technical sense, there seem to be some activities that are more clearly identified as teaching and instructing (i.e., classroom training), and others that seem more clearly aligned with what would be referred to as leadership (informal or formal influence upon others in the workplace).

The horizontal axis shows the concept of MI as an internal governance and development factor on the left, and an outward, other-focused dynamic on the right. This framework allows for four quadrants, which are Teaching-Inward (TI), Teaching-Outward (TO), Leading-Inward (LI), and Leading-Outward (LO). The inward dimensions are included as an acknowledgment that being a leader and an educator are life-wide and life-deep and are best done when they come from the heart and the whole person. The external behavior is rarely as powerful as it is when it extends from an authentic internal character.

Defined in this extended way, the following breakdown corresponds with Figure 4.1.

TI – The internal, critically reflective process of holding up every intended instructional action against every instructional intention. For each method employed in the practice of instruction, the instructor considers the intended short-term activity over and against the desired long-term outcome and ensures a "goodness of fit." Every act is an intentional and purposeful act, and at any moment, the instructor could share exactly why a particular method is used in a given context. Because of this, each action can be more accurately evaluated in terms of its intended long-term purpose. This is a sort of MEF of short-term action to long-term objective.

TO – The state of being in a moment-by-moment motivational relationship with the student. Defined as an *action process*, MI is the practice of purposefully adopting as a part of one's instructional method, the consistent, pervasive, and habitual attempt to connect with each individual learner and ensure that the learner is motivated in the immediate sense, regardless of whether global motivation is present or not.

LI – The internal, critically reflective process of holding up every intended daily activity and action and thought against one's long-term life goals for the purposes of ensuring a goodness of fit. This zone of MI is what has been referred to in this book as Reaching For behavior (see Chapter 5), and, because leadership is life-wide as well as lifelong, it requires the most powerful of leaders to apply it across the entirety of their life, at home and at work.

LO – MI can be seen as a *state* of being in a moment-by-moment motivational relationship with that one is leading. Defined as an *action process*, MI is the practice of purposefully adopting as a part of one's leadership method, the consistent, pervasive, and habitual attempt to connect with each individual learner and ensure that that those one is leading are motivated in the immediate sense, regardless of whether global motivation is present or not.

Effectual Learning

I said at the outset of this chapter that it would "draw all of the strings together" that were spun in the first three chapters. I also said that MI is a *junction*. It is the junction of where ideas become action, where theory becomes practice. It is the fulcrum over which the scale tips us toward street-level action rather than armchair epiphanies. An examination of the definition will reveal that it starts as a noun and ends as a verb. That is a good way to sum up what all applied science should look like – *it should start with a noun and end with a verb.*

What we are striving for in all of this effort is to facilitate effectual learning in the workplace, both informally and formally. I have tried to build a case here for the need for learning that includes both *acquisition* and *acceptance*, and after speaking and writing about this for a while I began to think of a way to encapsulate both of those factors together in a way that differentiated that type of learning with all of the other references to it that so often include only one. I use the term *effectual learning* to refer to any form of learning that includes both of these components.[14,15] The word effectual is very close in meaning to the similar, and more common word effective.

In digging a little on this, I found that while the words are very similar and many sources show them to be the same – with effectual being the more antiquated or obsolete term – there is a difference. Merriam-Webster provides a distinction in claiming that the word effective means "producing or capable of producing a result," while effectual "suggests the accomplishment of a desired result especially as viewed after the fact."[16]

Effectual then, seemed to fit very well with what I was trying to convey because the very reason I am speaking about learning that must include both acquisition and acceptance, is because it is the only way that learning will produce any sort of desired effect after the fact. This "after the fact" sort of effect is referred to by many different names, most notably in workplace literature, training transfer. The point is, the thing most all of us want but have so much trouble facilitating, is long-term, after the fact, behavior change. Again, no matter what one's theoretical position on training and learning, there is generally a consensus that the instructor wants some sort of lasting change in behavior – *after the fact.* It is this ultimate goal that has spurred the extensive body of literature related to the various aspects of training transfer.

My claim here, is that in order for this to happen, we must foster both acquisition and acceptance of the learning content, and I am therefore referring to learning where both of these dynamics are present as *effectual learning*.

Leading through Motivational Immediacy

What exactly does MI look like in leadership? We have spent some time addressing how there is a connection between teaching and leading and that is all well and good, but what about for those who are predominantly leaders, engaged in non-classroom, everyday organizational business? The first two chapters in the next section take up the mantel of the LI/LO domains of MI and address them in pretty direct ways. Chapter 5 addresses the specifics of MI in leadership practices, while Chapter 6 examines the workplace intersections of leading and teaching.

Notes

1 Taylor, J. E. (2022). *Motivational immediacy: Fostering engagement in adult learners*. Stylus.
2 Taylor, J. E. (2022). *Motivational immediacy in the workplace: Facilitating learner engagement in training environments*. Routledge.
3 Kruglanski, A. W., Fishback, A., Woolley, K., Belanger, J. J., Chernikova, M., Molinario, E., & Pierro, A. (2018). A structural model of intrinsic motivation: On the psychology of means-ends fusion. *Psychological Review*, *125*(2), 165–182. https://doi.org/10.1037/rev0000095
4 Kruglanski, A. W., Fishback, A., Woolley, K., Belanger, J. J., Chernikova, M., Molinario, E., & Pierro, A. (2018). A structural model of intrinsic motivation: On the psychology of means-ends fusion. *Psychological Review*, *125*(2), 165–182. https://doi.org/10.1037/rev0000095
5 Kruglanski, A. W., Fishback, A., Woolley, K., Belanger, J. J., Chernikova, M., Molinario, E., & Pierro, A. (2018). A structural model of intrinsic motivation: On the psychology of means-ends fusion. *Psychological Review*, *125*(2), 165–182. https://doi.org/10.1037/rev0000095
6 Taylor, J. E. (2022). *Motivational immediacy: Fostering engagement in adult learners*. Stylus.
7 Taylor, J. E. (2022). *Motivational immediacy in the workplace: Facilitating learner engagement in training environments*. New York.
8 Cabranes-Grant, L. (2018). Kierkegaard, Wagner and the quest for operatic immediacy. *The Wagner Journal*, *12*(1), 4–18.
9 Mehrabian, A. (1981). *Silent messages: Implicit communication of emotions and attitudes* (2nd ed.). Wadsworth Publishing Company, Inc.
10 Burroughs, N. F. (2007). A reinvestigation of the relationship of teacher nonverbal immediacy and student compliance-resistance with learning. *Communication Education*, *56*(4), 453–475. https://doi.org.10.1080/03634520701530896

11 Burroughs, N. F. (2007). A reinvestigation of the relationship of teacher nonverbal immediacy and student compliance-resistance with learning. *Communication Education*, *56*(4), 453–475. https://doi.org.10.1080/03634520701530896
12 Taylor, J. E. (2022). *Motivational immediacy: Fostering engagement in adult learners.* Stylus.
13 Taylor, J. E. (2022). *Motivational immediacy in the workplace: Facilitating learner engagement in training environments.* New York.
14 Taylor, J. E. (2022). *Motivational immediacy: Fostering engagement in adult learners.* Stylus.
15 Taylor, J. E. (2022). *Motivational immediacy in the workplace: Facilitating learner engagement in training environments.* New York.
16 Merriam Webster Dictionary. www.merriam-webster.com/dictionary/effectual

Section II

Practicing Motivational Immediacy

Chapter 5

Motivational Immediacy in Leadership

The widely popular serenity prayer attributed to Reinhold Niebuhr in the early 1930s continues to share its truth from the quilts, books, and walls of homes all over the world. More than 2000 years before Niebuhr's words, the Greek Stoic philosopher Epictetus wrote much the same – human beings can control very little in our lives in consistently definitive ways. What we can control, however, is how we choose to process the events we experience, and the attitudes and philosophies we choose to develop and guide us. Modern psychology has shown us that the attitudes we adapt, our dispositions regarding our everyday experiences, are one of the most powerful pathways to continued peace of mind and mental health.

Motivational Immediacy-Leadership

Motivational immediacy on the internal leadership side (LI as depicted in Figure 5.1) is a purposeful act to engage mental energy toward means-end fusion (MEF). By always keeping the desired ends in sight, and mentally holding any present act (and thought) as the means, up against the desired ends, two things happen. First, one can remain excited about a goal and steadfast in pursuit of a goal, even if there is quite a long tedious journey before that end is achieved. Second, by purposefully fusing means and ends as a routinely engaged mental habit, one can better ensure that any given action (and thought) is, in fact, actually in effective and efficient service of the ends. This act of mental MEF is what I am referring to as "Reaching For."

Reasons Why We Should Be Motivational Immediate in Leadership (Reach For)

1. Make sure we remain consistently motivated – Avoid ambivalence.
2. Make sure we remain appropriately motivated – Avoid philosophical ambiguity.
3. Make sure we remain Precisely motivated – avoid "mission creep."

DOI: 10.4324/9781003482079-7

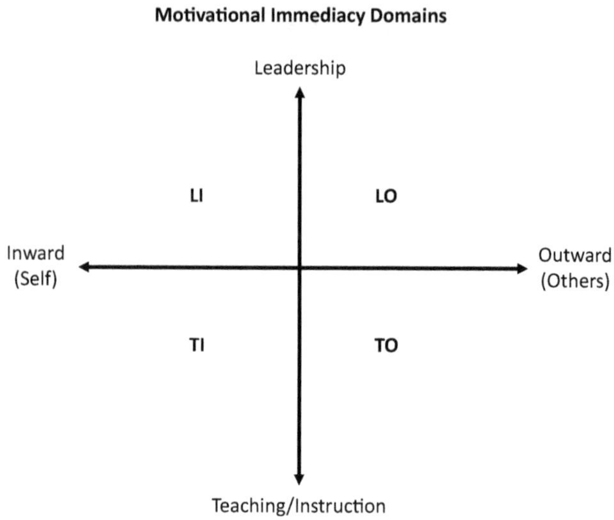

Figure 5.1 Motivational Immediacy Zones.

One often hears that one should not "react" to problems. This is good advice, but it is also problematic, as all good advice is, when you feel around the edges of it. It creates a false binary in which we either react – typically in a rash and emotive way – or we respond – typically with greater thought and more calmness. In truth though, a given response may or may not be appropriate whether it is emotionally charged or not. Most of us have made singularly bad decisions at some point or another even after thinking about it and being calm while making it. Our well-thought calm decisions may also consist of a range of actions which may or may not be healthy, helpful, or even ethical. Rash response is not the only risk we face. Motivational immediacy breaks down options into the four following options: Reacting to, Running From, Repeating of, and Reaching For.

This chapter connects the idea of motivational immediacy and leadership to the action orientation of *Reaching For* and provides some practical examples of what these look like and how they may play out. After this, some simple steps are provided to properly analyze situations and to choose a reaching for orientation to leadership.

The Four R's

When faced with any live event, or any set of complex social dynamics, we are faced with four choices for viewing the path ahead of us. We can react to it, we can run from it, we can repeat it, or we can reach for it. In reality, we often do a strange mix of all of these things, resulting in a conflicted, inefficient, and unsettling way forward.

Running from something is probably the easiest to write about in ways that we can all understand because it is something that we all tend to do. One need not watch too many movies or read too many books to hear a theme embedded somewhere in there that an otherwise good choice turns out badly because the protagonist was making it in an attempt to run away from some other thing. It is a classic case of a doing a good thing for the wrong reasons.

Reacting to something is a second way we can respond to a life event. I almost wrote "can choose to respond" but that would have been misleading because it makes it sound as though we make these decisions in conscious and thoughtful and intentional ways. In everyday life, sadly, we don't. We rummage around in the forest without any real reflection of why we are pressing on in the direction we are going other than some vague, unchallenged impression that we are heading for something we want or need. When we react to something, we are, in a fundamental way, giving up personal control of the decisions we make, the directions we take, and the types of results we are likely to get.

Repeating of is likely something we do from the weakest of all human positions. It is not a decision to be something we say, to repeat something we liked, it is a developmental accident where we unintentionally become that very thing, or cause that very thing, that we ourselves were exposed to somewhere in our past. When we repeat something, we are becoming something without critical self-reflection, without clear thought, without purpose, and without intention. We are, very much like a leaf floating in a stream, going where it goes, becoming what it becomes with no individual agency.

An example of this might be some of the negative behaviors, habits, or practices that we picked up from those we were exposed to earlier in life. In the instructional world, it is not uncommon to see new instructors mimic some of the very training behaviors they have complained about for years when they were the learner rather than the teacher. There are, of course, those who end up "becoming their parents" later in life. More serious examples of repeating might be harmful behaviors and unhealthy mental habits that were learned from others early in life and never critiqued with purpose.

Reaching for is the most powerful way to approach a situation in life, and the only way to live with full, actualized, personal agency and the fullest human dignity. It is to live life in a way that every single action is an act of intentionality. It is the mental habit of ensuring that whatever one is doing, they are doing it to reach in a positive way toward some goal that they are sure they want.

The point here is not about *what* goals should be chosen, nor do all goals have to be large and of great importance. Some more significant life situations will be discussed below, but first it is worth pointing out that reaching for (motivational immediacy) can be practiced in all of the little decisions that are made in life also. Being intentional does not mean that one cannot relax, let loose, and just have fun. On the contrary, there will be space for more of all of those things. For instance, one might decide to go out to dinner with a friend or spouse but then feel guilty about the money being spent and work being left undone. This is a distraction and the negativity erodes some of the positive ends that were sought. Conversely, if one is going to go to dinner with a friend or a spouse, taking a few minutes to determine why one wants to do this – what specific ends are sought – and then to keep that present *in the moment* throughout the entire event, is a healthy choice. It will typically keep one's focus off of negative aspects and on the positive reasons the decision was made to begin with. In this case, the diner will bask in its positive moments and will be more fun and healthier. And, it will have the added benefit of making you better company for whoever you are at dinner with.

Moving on to what might be considered larger-scale and more life-altering decisions, I will briefly share two examples.

The Dreaded Customer Review

From the perspective a small business owner, there is nearly nothing that induces more dread than the prospect of getting a bad review on any of the primary public domains, social media platforms, and advertising hubs. It may be a concern for large business owners as well, but it simply cannot bring the fear factor experienced by those in small businesses all over the country. Without having decades of name-brand cultural embeddedness, and a production volume robust enough to weather temporary trends, single proprietor business and "mom and pop" operations the world over must rely on the good impressions and good will of virtually anyone who happens by (regardless of whether or not the reviewer is even a client to begin with). For those lucky enough to have made it a year or two into their venture with only positive reviews, the anxiety is, perhaps, even worse – waiting, wondering when the first devastating customer review will put an end to their life's dream.

There are a few different developmental stages along the way for those who are moving from new business owner to more experienced, veteran business owner. Although it is certain than all business owners do not experience life the same way, or respond in similar fashion, there are some useful generalities that can be made. The following description of two different ways to view and approach customer reviews is a very good way to illuminate the difference between the *running from* and *reaching for* constructs being discussed here. Keep in mind, though, that the ideas of reaching for and running from match very closely the psychological constructs of approach motivation and avoidance motivation.

A personal experience may help demonstrate an everyday life application. After purchasing a small event venue a few years ago, it immediately became apparent that bad customer reviews would seriously hurt our business, which, of course, translates to not being able to pay the bills. Not being able to pay the bills results in (fore)closure. Because of this apparent truth, we began immediately to adopt a "do not get a bad review" approach to business.

It is difficult, at first, to see the error in this way of thinking. After all, going back to our idea of street-smarts, it has served us well in many ways, as an adaptive strategy throughout life. We all know that burn injuries are terribly painful and harmful or fatal, and therefore, we adopt a strategy to make our way through daily life by avoiding burns. That is, we often know what we don't want with a great deal more clarity than what we do want. And, avoiding the thing we know we don't want, does seem to keep us from experiencing the thing we don't want, at least much of the time. Because of this daily confirmation of our applied strategy, we expand it and adapt it and utilize it across the board, to nearly all areas of life. Taken to its extreme, however, we avoid the pain of burns, but also the peaceful joy of campfires. We avoid the terrible death fire can bring but also the wonderful life it can render. This sort of thinking ends up being what I would call an epistemological rut. A rut is something you slide into and then can't get out of without significant effort. The problem here (like many problems in life) has at its bottom a false dichotomy. We can avoid burns by fires by practicing safe practices *with* fires. In so doing, we enjoy the best while also avoiding the worst.

Going back to customer reviews after that short digression with fire, one tends to think that seeking to avoid a bad review is the best way to avoid getting a bad review. Like the fire example above, it is an effective way to run from a bad review, but accomplishes only that – the avoidance of the bad with none of the good.

In our own small business, we worked tremendously hard to avoid bad reviews and, in the end, after our initial two years, pulled it off. And, what we had was exactly that – no bad reviews. However, somewhere along the line, as we continued in our work and continued in our learning, we came to realize a few things. First, we realized that ultimately, eventually, we would get a bad review no matter what we did. That is just a reality of the world of people and of social interactions among people.

Second, we started looking at the reviews of other small businesses and noticed a few things. We noticed that although nearly every business that had been around long enough had a few bad reviews, what mattered most was (a) how many reviews they had, and (b) what percentage of them were good vs. bad. So, a business with 331 reviews might have 4.5 out of 5 stars, even though there were a few negative reviews.

Some quick checking found that with enough reviews, a near 5-star average is possible even in the face of a scathing review or two. Using a common online review calculator (there really is such a thing!), a full seven 1-star reviews (the "big guns" for bad reviews – these people have serious problems with you), in the face of one thousand 5-star reviews, comes out to a 4.96-star rating. One thousand 5-star, five 4-star, and two 1-star reviews leave you with a very strong 4.987.

This is pretty powerful, mathematically speaking. Getting lots of good reviews makes the bad reviews not all that important. But much more powerful than the actual math involved is the qualitative data of the reader seeing positive, very descriptive review after review while having to scroll down quite a ways to see one dissenting (and often nasty) remark by someone. It may or may not be a legitimate complaint, but the optics are clearly in the favor of the business owner if there are many very specific and strong reviews available to peruse.

As the second-year unfolded into the third, we began to realize that we needed to drop our quest to run from bad reviews, and instead, adopt a new quest to earn (reach for) as many good reviews as possible. As this process has unfolded for us, anecdotally, we have learned the following:

Avoiding bad reviews fosters the following potentially problematic behaviors (and resultant errors):

1. Being averse to saying no to customers under any circumstances. At best, this creates a situation in which the business owner is simply doing what must be done to keep someone happy (often after they already are not). At worst, this behavior results in decisions that are harmful for the business, the facilities, the employees, and also sometimes the customers themselves (e.g., okay, you can have a fire in your hotel room, just this once).
2. Being obsessed with running from bad reviews, can foster a weak, "wishy-washy" routine of interactions with customers. Things that were "no" become "yes" or, perhaps worse, "maybe" portraying an image of insecurity and a lack of experience and professionalism. Constant negotiated changes to policy out of fear can also send the signal that there were not good reasons behind the decisions to begin with (which means there may not be good reasons behind any of the other rules, policies, etc., either).

3. Avoiding bad reviews does absolutely nothing to get you any good ones. With many good ones, you can mitigate the effects of the eventual bad one you will get. With no reviews at all, you are not considered a viable professional entity to begin with. One might even agree that a controversial identity is preferable to no identity at all. "Who is this business? Are they legit?"

On the flip side, when dropping the bad review avoidance completely and, instead, reaching for good reviews, passionately and ardently, the following positive benefits naturally follow:

1. The business owner is thinking at all times about how the customer might be best served.
2. The business owner only makes rules and policies to begin with that are absolutely required to avoid damage, harm, or excessive liability, and then sticks to them unless there is a very reasonable exception.
3. The business owner is always thinking of new ways to build customer satisfaction and confidence.
4. The business owner is always thinking of rules as a way to ensure the possible positive outcome rather than avoiding some potential negative outcome.

Looking at these two sets of tendencies, one can see the following contrasts:

1. Running from leaves us avoiding the worst, while reaching for has us striving for the best.
2. Running from leaves us indecisive and weak, while reaching for allows us to be clear and strong.
3. Running from leaves us ultimately with some of what we didn't want and little of what we did, while reaching for gives us lots of what we wanted, less of what we didn't, and less negative effects from the latter when we do get it.
4. Running from results in the thing we dread being more powerful, while reaching for leaves the thing we are dreading remote, isolated, and inert.

Building Consensus or Protecting Insecurity

The second example is a personal reflection of a situation in which I came to see that I had been running from something instead of reaching for something. At the end of this story, I was still engaging in the same practices, but doing so with a much better motive, with greater skill, and with a much more powerful reach.

Throughout my entire career, and likely even before that, I had a particular ability to find consensus with others and build on it. This is a skill that developed over time and became part of how I thought of myself in terms of my relationship to others and to personal and professional life. While my skills certainly developed over time and with social experience, I think it is fair to say that that particular skill, or the tendency that engendered it, is at least partially innate. This has served me well in my professional life, particularly, because everyday experience would lead one to believe there is a dearth of natural consensus builders out there, and also because it allowed me to facilitate opportunities that have brought very different sorts of people together with a common goal. When it comes off cleanly (and sometimes it doesn't), consensus building provides a field for everyone in the group to benefit and grow together (and I have grown too). Over time, I have come to feel pretty good about this skill, maybe because I don't feel like I have many other good social skills, but partly because it *feels* good to feel good at something.

This is a success story so far and might lead the reader to begin to think it is a bit of self-aggrandizement. But there is a point to my story, and it is not my consensus building acumen, such that it may or may not be. The narrative changed rather sharply when, in the midst of middle age (I am being kind to myself there) my professional life situation changed in a tremendously significant way but one in which only someone who knows my history well would know. I ended up entering into a period of professional interactions that forced my hand in uncomfortable ways. Simply put, for the first time in my life, I was in a position where I was forced to have a sustained professional position that required that I disagree overtly, chronically, and pervasively. That is, there was no space that I could find to build consensus. I simply had to take a series of stands, all of them for prolonged periods, where I was the odd man out. I was the person in the way of progress, the impediment, the obstacle. During this period, I believed that I had the moral high ground and didn't have much of a choice, but my point here is not at all about whether I was right in my stand, but what the experience exposed to me about my personality and the social practices that had become habituated over many years.

Having no space to build consensus, I was forced to think long and hard about what that meant for me, which made me think about my social inclinations. What I found is that although consensus building was a good thing to do, and a great skill to have, my reason for it was not necessarily a good motivation to have or a great indicator of inner strength. What I figured out was that from a very early age, I developed a habit of finding ways to avoid having anyone disagree with me, while still managing to avoid compromising my own viewpoints. On the upside, I never had a tendency to compromise my moral views for others, but on the significant downside, I did focus my attention on how to render a situation into one that everyone got along with me and thought I was pretty okay. Put bluntly, my consensus building skill and eventual way of being, was born out of something as simple and unflattering as personal insecurity. It was about me. It was defensive. And, to the point here, it was birthed from a drive to *run from* a feeling of social disapproval. I run the risk here of spending too much space talking about myself, but I think it is a good example of the larger point because the behavior was a good behavior, the outcomes were good outcomes, and the general skill is sought after in the professional and personal world. But the motivation for the behavior was not so positive.

The period of having to be at odds with many of my colleagues and to take a "last stand" passed quickly enough (it did not seem quick at the time), but the epiphany continued to grow. A big question I started mulling over was this – what would happen if I applied that same skill, with passion and energy with a motive to improve the given situation and bring about positive change in those around me? What if I applied that skill free from personal insecurity? What If I applied that skill with expansive, reckless abandon to improve the situation for everyone around me, myself included? Reaching for is a more powerful way to live.

A Few Takeaways

- *Running From* is avoidance motivation, while *Reaching For* is approach motivation (as discussed in Chapter 2). Approach motivation is healthier in many ways than avoidance motivation, even if the external practical results are exactly the same. Therefore, reaching for is more conducive to personal health than running from.
- Although the original motivator for a conduct may not be a healthy one, good, adaptive, and beneficial behaviors and skills can develop out of it.
- The point of *Reaching For* is not to be harshly critical about the past, but to be powerfully proactive for the future. The goal is to harness more power from what you may already be doing; to engage more fully with others and to extend your reach in significant ways while being a healthier person, mentally and physically.

Even a Rebel can Run From...

H. A. Williams, over 50 years ago, wrote about a type of rebel who is actually a conformist.[1] Williams' point was something quite different from the overall thrust of this book but was quite in line with the idea of reaching for rather than running from, or repeating of. He demonstrates how complicated it can get trying to determine whether someone is reaching for or running from. He wrote that,

> A man may be a rebel, for instance, because he has fire in his belly and wishes to change what he considers wrong with the world. If so, in his rebellion he is being and becoming himself. *[this would be reaching for]* But rebellion can [also] be no more than the enactment of a role or a counter-role. As counter-role it is a reaction against the attempted imposition of roles in childhood. *[this would be running from]* Or a man may find himself caught up in a community where rebellion is expected of him. Then it is a role. *[this would be repeating of]* It is as a rebel that he is accepted and valued. In these circumstances rebellion is a mode of conformity. It is by playing the part of a rebel that he purchases membership of the group. But he seldom sees the trick which has been played upon him. He sincerely believes he is on fire for the cause. And he is content that for the sake of the cause his humanity should wither away… the role of the rebel is eventually exchanged for the role of the establishment [person].

He goes on to write that,

> "here again a distinction must be made. If a society has made possible the growth and flowering of a [person's] abilities and personality, then [their] attempts to preserve the structure of [their] alma mater are the means whereby [they] are and become [themselves]. *[reaching for]* But people can be strong establishment [people] in order to feel that they belong to its elite. They are pillars of society in order to feel that they are pillars. They murder their essential self because they feel more secure as impressive brass. *[Running from]*.

Approach vs. Avoidance Motivation

Taking all of this back to the previous discussions about psychology and motivation, what we see above is avoidance motivation and approach motivation. Each can result in the motivated behavior being evoked, but one is powerful and healthy, while the other has been shown to be weak and sickly.

Reaching For and Motivational Immediacy

Motivational immediacy here, then, is the practice (habit of mind and body) to at all times, keep the ultimate reach for out in front of us, and to craft, locate, and evaluate every single short-term action to the long-term desire.

Keeping the short-term action viewed over and against the long-term goal in a moment-by-moment dynamic will keep us focused on the right thing, increase our chances of accomplishing the most good, and achieving and maintaining sound mental and physical health while doing it.

This particular definition of motivational immediacy can be found in the upper left quadrant of Figure 5.1 – Leadership/Inward. It is on the leadership end of the spectrum because it concerns goal setting, agenda construction, and policy formation. It is on the internal end of the spectrum because it has to do with the internal workings of external determinations and proclamations. It is about the *why* behind the decision, not the decision itself. The why is a deeply personal thing and therefore positioned on the inward side of the figure.

Note

1 Williams, H. A. (1972). *True resurrection* (p. 107). Harper & Row.

Chapter 6

What Are We Doing Here?

Zones of Leadership, Mentoring, and Training

It is a nearly universal truth that to take something out of its natural habitat is to make it significantly less natural. There may or may not be harm in something being less natural, but there is tremendous risk in losing sight of what it naturally *is* and, instead, coming to see its newly conceptualized state as the "new natural." This is true of animals in the zoo, but it is true also of something much more present in our everyday lives – learning.

Any attempt to harness human learning, in the form of human teaching, and to place artificial structure to it, facilitates a "new natural" for learning that we have, as a species, largely fallen into without even realizing it. We have confused how we so often *do* education, with what education actually, in the natural (and most optimal) world, really *is*. This has not been all bad, of course, and working to bring wildly organic, natural phenomena into a more predictable, and therefore usable, entity, makes a lot of sense. The real harm is in not being aware that what we have done to it, has also changed what we often think of it as being. This chapter is intended to bring our focus back to exactly what human learning, as a naturally occurring phenom, is. This matters because we spend so much time and money trying to figure out how to do it best. We need to work with the real natural as well as the new natural. We may find that things do not need to be as they so often are.

The natural phenomenon of learning, that is, as it exists and appears in an organic sense, has two qualities about it that are not only often ignored, but most of the time actually denied. The first is that learning and leading are powerfully connected in ways that naturally cause both to be diminished when either is ignored. The second is that learning takes place at all times and in all places and therefore teaching is, whether we like it or not, whether we acknowledge it or not, and even whether we believe it or not, taking place at all times and in all places also. If leading and teaching are so deeply connected, as I believe the evidence indicates that they are, then leading is also taking place at all times and in all places. The practical implications of this are immense.

DOI: 10.4324/9781003482079-8

Leading and Teaching

One of the bolder assumptions in this book is that teaching, instruction, and leading are all a part of the same overarching activity in the workplace. That may seem, at first glance, like a bit of a heavy lift, but this chapter, more than any other, will show the deep and abiding connection between the two. In order to be able to identify and understand all of the teaching and leadership spaces in the workplace, one must be able to first identify and understand all of the learning spaces within the workplace, which I have referred to previously both as the zones of intervention,[1] and the zones of motivational immediacy,[2,3] but am here referring to as zones of leadership, mentoring, and teaching.

There are doubtless many nuanced arguments that can be engaged in about all of the gray areas between what might constitute teaching and what might constitute leading. The core view being stressed here sidesteps most of this and addresses a solid middle area of overlap that can be expressed in this statement: Anyone who is effectively leading is teaching something to someone, and anyone who is effectively teaching anything to anyone is extending leadership to someone in some area of their lives and within some limited context at the time of the event. This dual statement is difficult to refute given the empirical work on each and the definitions of each. There is a practical truth obvious here as well. It is the implications of this limited but important statement that are the focus of the motivational immediacy concepts discussed here.

Before beginning, there is a key distinction to be made. Although I *am* making the claim that leading is a form of teaching (and of course learning), I am *not* claiming that leading represents all types of teaching and learning equally, or at all times. That is, I am making the case that the essence of leadership is teaching, and that the essence of teaching is leading, but I am not speaking for the very specific sub-skills required by both leaders and teachers for those specific domains. Being a leader in a large company does not mean that one is properly trained and equipped to teach a third-grade class or an undergraduate course, and being a third-grade or undergraduate teacher does not automatically qualify someone for effective leading in the workplace. Each of these domains of professional practice has its own required skills and this book makes no claim of "one size fits all." These distinctions, however, do not detract from an epic truth that hinders workplace leaders – *leading is, among other things, the facilitation of learning in others.*

All of this might sound pedantic and academic, but it is of a sheerly practical concern. Because of the failure to see the substantial overlap between the two, the papers and books written about each steer clear of the brilliant practice and scholarship of the other. So, to be clear, this is a book on teaching and learning and is meant to open new worlds of effective practice for workplace leaders. It is not merely one more book on leadership.

Leadership as Seen through an Educational Lens

One of the significant challenges in looking at definitions of leadership related concepts is that unlike words such as learning and teaching, which are stated and defined most often as action-oriented words, the word *leading* is hard to find at all. A brief search on any platform will confirm this almost instantly. And, to make it worse, while one can easily find definitions of the act of teaching *and* the act of learning (i.e., teachers and learners), it is nearly impossible to find a good characterization of those who follow leaders. The term leading is difficult to find with a definition, but the word "follower" in this context is not popular at all, and this makes sense because most of us would not opt to be referred to as a follower, which of course, has other negative connotations.

There is a somewhat recent move to refer (and sometimes define) leadership as a group dynamic,[4] and although this likely has some redeeming value, it does tend to avoid the basic truth that a leader does in fact want others to follow the lead. Again, this can seem like hairsplitting, but it is not, because in the case of the teaching and learning literature ample time and attention (theory, research, analysis) are devoted to (a) the act of teaching, (b) the act of learning, and (c) the interaction of the two. The collaborative nature of the teaching and learning process has not been overlooked in the recent decades despite having a clear sense of learners and teachers as related but distinct. This collaboration, however, has *not* brought about a move to stop talking about the learner.

Scholarship on the topic of leadership has gone a different, less healthy route. It has avoided talking about those who are led in any real sense and simply focuses on how to be a leader and inspire others. The problem with this is that leading, like teaching, is only and always about the *other*. Only being able to address leadership from the perspective of the leader leaves out a great deal of very useful information that could be used to improve the workplace for those who are leading as well as those who are being led in any given circumstance.

The power of what I am sharing here, in this present analysis, is that when one focuses on leading as the facilitation of learning (even if the leader is learning also), one is able to pay close attention to both the leader (as teacher) and the one who is supposed to be led (as learner). It is disingenuous to deny that there is a clear division between who is supposed to be facilitating the most directional leadership and who is supposed to be led by that leadership. It may be true that we are all leaders in this domain or that, and we ought not think of one person only as the leader in a global sense, but we cannot deny the real-world truth that at whatever moment someone is actually leading, someone else is actually being led. Going forward in this chapter, I *am referring to leadership in essence, as the facilitation of a particular kind of learning in a specific learner or group of learners, in a specific situation or context.* I do not intend for this to be a watertight definition or even one that is useful in all circumstances. However, using this definition will open up vast areas of growth for the leader in the workplace to increase in capacity, efficiency, and influential power.

John C. Maxwell refers to leadership as simply "influence."[5] If influence is broadly considered to be having an effect on the behavior or development of another, it is very closely aligned with the idea of teaching. The Center for Creative Leadership explains leadership this way:

> Leadership means different things to different people, but is often widely considered as the ability to influence, motivate, and enable others to contribute toward the effectiveness and success of the organisation or group. It's about *inspiring a shared vision, setting clear goals, and creating an environment where people can thrive and achieve their full potential* (emphasis added).[6]

Inspiring people to adopt a shared vision and to set specific goals for accomplishing the mission is significantly educative and instructional. Creating an environment that is conducive to personal development is also educative, and large volumes of educational research and theory have been focused on these areas.

Again, although one can make certain distinctions between the two, there is undoubtably a great intertwining of the two in the workplace that can be demonstrated by looking at the learning (and leading) spaces that exist there. Two particular theories of learning are in close alignment with the act of providing leadership, and I will share them here before moving on to examine workplace learning and leading spaces.

Learning in All Places and at All Times

Jean Lave and Etienne Wenger perhaps more than anyone else, disrupted the idea that learning occurs entirely in an abstract, sterile, and "unsituated" way.[7,8,9] They and others have insisted that learning is entirely embedded in the social milieu and is inseparable from its context. Wenger's[10,11] conception of learning as a dynamic that is bounded by a community of practice in which the learner experiences learning as *belonging*, learning as *becoming*, learning as *experiencing*, and learning as *doing* leads one to fully consider that authentic learning is perhaps always connected in some way to mentorship and to leadership. There is also the implication that learning may take place at all times and in all quarters of the workplace learning space.

If this is the case – that is, that employees are learning at all times in every facet of the workplace, then it must further be considered that learning is also being *facilitated* at all times and in every facet of the workplace. Going further if learning is being facilitated at all times, than leadership is also being exerted at all times and in all places.

Leading and, by extension, leadership, has been subject to the same colloquial distortion as motivation (discussed in Chapter 2). Somehow, the term leadership has come to most often refer, in a common sense sort of way, to *positive* leading. It is true that we know better, technically speaking, but even when the term "bad leadership" or "poor leadership" is used, we most often are referring to leadership that is weak and not practically very helpful. That is, we tend to think leadership is a positive notion in general that some people sometimes do poorly.

Leadership, however, like motivation, can be a very good thing or a very bad thing, depending who is being led by whom, and where. We seem to understand that someone can lead informally just by being "followable" but the emphasis still seems to largely be on purposeful action toward something good. This can be a positive viewpoint for sure, but it has the terribly harmful effect of leading us to believe that there are spaces and times at work where leadership is not being exerted and that is simply not the case. To miss this aspect of reality will result in always being brought up short when striving for excellence in workplace leadership. Halftime is over and the game has started and we are in our office having a cup of coffee wondering why are aren't earning the most valuable player.

A little further on, I will share that learning in the workplace takes place in four overlapping zones. What may be surprising is that our "go to" for workplace learning, might actually be the weakest and least effective of the four.

Danish Educational Psychologist Knud Illeris[12] speaks of two axes of learning, the *acquisition* and the *interaction*. The acquisition axis is in a reciprocal relationship between what he refers to as the content dimension (knowledge, understanding, skills), and the incentive dimension (motivation, emotion, and volition). These internal dynamics, together making up the acquisition process, also interact in a reciprocal fashion, with the external environment. This meeting of the individual with the environment, Illeris refers to as the interaction process. The interaction process connects the individual learner with the social nature of learning, which results in the third dimension of learning (social). The external environment (social), which is made up of both the social (localized social situation) as well as the societal, encompasses all of the extant theory on social aspects of learning while, in a more holistic sense sees these social dynamics as inseparable from the internal processes.

In a workplace learning adaption of his original perspective on the dimensions of learning, Illeris substituted the environmental side of the figure with social dimensions in line with the workplace learning spaces. Instead of *social* and *sociality*, he includes *production* on the one side, and *community* on the other, referring, respectively, to the dynamics involved with the purpose of the workplace itself – production, and the general social situation as it is altered by being bounded, at least to a certain extent, by the workplace. These ideas do not venture far from his ideas in conceptual terms but provide added levels of specificity for the workplace learning space.

The importance of this explanation of human learning is first that its complexity brings it into sharper focus within the domain of providing leadership and influence in the workplace. Additionally, in order for all educational and leadership opportunities to be clearly recognized and utilized in efforts to improve the workplace for both the employer and employee alike, all dimensions of human learning must be acknowledged and understood. The zones suggested below are, in fact, simply the logical conclusion of zooming out on the learning and leading process and seeing all of its many different dynamics, not the least of which are cognitive, affective, and social.

Looking at Wenger and Illeris together leads up to a very basic understanding about the ever-present characteristic of human learning. If this is the case, and we wish to foster engagement in employee learners in the workplace, then we must be motivationally immediate at all times and in all places as well.

The Four Zones of Leadership, Mentoring, and Teaching

One way the workplace learning spaces can be depicted is by dividing the entire workplace learning space into four zones, developed by the quadrants of a vertical and horizontal axis. Figure 6.1 shows the following four poles on two axes: Individual Context vs. Organizational Context and Classroom Leadership vs. Community Leadership. Taking both Illeris'[13] and Wenger's[14,15] depictions of workplace learning as complicated integrations of personal, organizational, and environmental factors, and assuming that as such, such learning is generally not bounded by the walls of a classroom, the zones presented here represent four "distinct" spaces in which leading and learning take place continually in the workplace.

Context Axis

Looking first at the context axis (Figure 6.1), one can see that it extends in a range from the ***individual context*** on the top end, to the ***organizational context*** on the bottom end. These poles are meant to show the polar ends of the construct for the sake of analytical clarity. It is important to realize that in everyday life there is overlap and the lines are considerably less clear. The poles are important, however, because they expose the outer limits of the zones of learning that we all experience every day.

Simply put, the individual context refers here to individual learning as distinct from organizational factors. It places focus on the internal cognition of individual leaners in the workplace and how those learners interpret and process information and social interaction.

The organizational context, on the other hand, focuses specifically on the organization as a whole and the collective learning process of the employees.

Individual Context. The individual context, as noted above, places emphasis on the individual learning processes and, in keeping with this, on teaching methods and processes as they address the learner on an individual learner, distinct from the more socially oriented organizational aspects of learning.

Organizational Context. While the individual context focuses on the internal processes as they interact with the environment, the organizational context focuses specifically on the organization as a whole and the collective

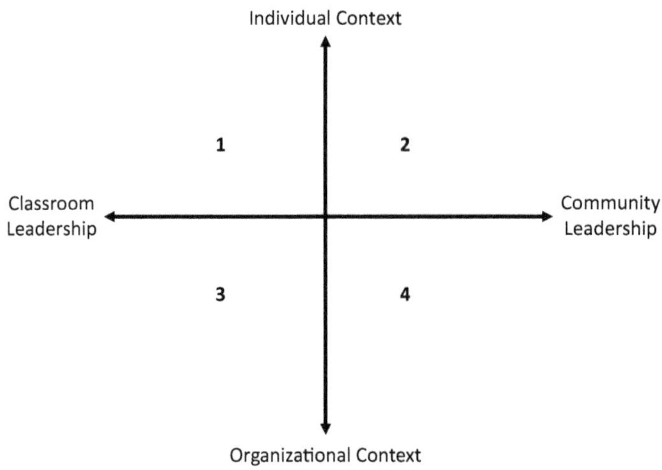

Figure 6.1 The Zones of Leadership, Mentoring, and Teaching.

learning process of the employees. This is similar in many ways to informal learning ideas.[16]

Classroom Leadership: An attempt to solve a problem through classroom training.
Community Leadership: An attempt to solve a problem through changes in the workplace community.
Individual Context: Used here to indicate a focus on solving a problem through addressing the behaviors and effects of individual employees.
Organizational Context: Used here to indicate a focus on solving the problem through addressing the dynamics, phenomena, and effects of the organization (i.e., systems and culture).

Leadership Axis

Classroom Leadership. Classroom instruction and leadership is facilitated through classroom training. This is the standard approach to solving workplace problems through education and training. It is important to note here that the word classroom does not necessarily refer to an actual room, in the traditional sense, but includes that format along with online and blended training courses in the workplace. This form of intervention typically arises because management either identifies a problem of some type or determines a learning goal for members of the organization and then determines that the need can be addressed through employee training.

This zone has the characteristic of being the most often employed but also the most limited form of leading and instruction in the workplace. It may be surprising to think of this as the place where the absolute smallest percentage of any workplace learning takes place, but that is exactly the case. Remember from the motivated *not* to learn chapter that one of the reasons employees often refuse to engage in workplace training is because what they are hearing is so starkly at odds with what they are learning from all of the other areas of workplace learning (i.e., everyday experience). On top of this, if learning is taking place 100% of the time, then the very limited number of actual classroom training hours shows just how little of the total percentage of learning is taking place in this area.

Community Leadership. A community intervention is an attempt to solve a problem or foster the development of employees through changes in the workplace community/organization. This type of intervention is also commonly used and is therefore not a "new" intervention, per se. Efforts along these lines are usually represented by workplace signage, programs, awareness campaigns, and employee reward systems. Taking these four poles of the vertical and horizontal axis into account, the presence of four quadrants comes into focus.

Workplace Zones of Leadership and Teaching

The two axes identified above form four zones in which the interaction of the two axis poles create a set of dynamics that have significant implications for those who wish to make full use of all educational, training, and leading opportunities in the workplace. The four zones are (1) applying a classroom approach to address the individual context, (2) applying a community approach to address the individual context, (3) applying a classroom approach to address the organizational context, and (4) applying a community approach to address the organizational context. *All four of these zones are spaces in which learner engagement can be fostered and in which motivational immediacy must be present.*

Zone 1: Classroom Approach–Individual Context. To ground these ideas, an example can be used in which a company determines that unsafe practices exist within the organization, as evidenced by large numbers of employee accidents and injuries. In an effort to change these practices, a workplace-wide training program is "rolled out" providing information on safety practices, appropriate and inappropriate behaviors at work, and processes by which an individual can work more safely. This is a typical method for addressing a very typical problem in production industries. One can easily envision the horrific videos and pictures that employees may be exposed to in such a training course for the purpose of driving home a need to avoid certain practices (e.g., leaving protective guard plates off of machinery) and to adopt others (e.g., wearing eye protection). By attempting to apply an intervention in a formal classroom structure while operating from an individual context, those making the decision are operating on a basic set of assumptions. For instance, one must assume that formalized class or course structures are an effective method for changing the behavior of employees over time; that there is some sort of long-term training transfer. Also, there must be an assumption that changing individuals is the way to change the community.

Zone 2: Community Approach–Individual Context. Continuing with the safety problem above, an example of this type of intervention would be a situation in which the company decided to promote an awareness campaign in which signage was posted throughout the workplace, and emails were sent out to everyone promoting safety practices and discouraging unsafe problems. Again, just about everyone has seen this type of "buckle-up" campaign in the workplace in some form or another. Both this zone and the previous zone have in common the focus on the addressing the problem through the context of the *individual.* Assumptions implicit with this approach are that this type of marketing style education will be effective with the organization's employees (i.e., they will read them and internalize them), and, like the previous zone, that change is best sought through the individual employee.

Zone 3: Classroom Approach–Organizational Context. Like Zone 1, Zone 3 uses the classroom or structured course setting to address problems. The difference here is that the organizational context is taken into account when developing the content and focus for the educational course. Carrying forward the safety training from above, the approach would be to "teach" or "train" employees about the safety problems and the necessity to eliminate such practices in the workplace. But in this case, rather than just addressing the harmful practices that need to stop and the safe practices that need to replace them, the course will focus on the system and structural causes of unsafe practices, and also the ways a workplace can engender such behaviors *structurally* and *organizationally* (similar in some ways to Argyris & Schon's double-loop learning[17]). For example, if employees of a package delivery service are told to sign a policy indicating that they are not to walk on the conveyor belts while they are moving, but then are placed in workplace situations where no other option is available (i.e., stopping the belts jams up the entire process for a large number of workers and the production process itself), they will very likely go the practical route rather than the policy route. Again, this is consistent with Lave and Wenger's[18] ideas of learning within a community. Since this is also a classroom intervention, employees would be asked to participate and discuss the factors that might lead them to engage in the unsafe practices in question. They might further be asked to collaborate to identify solutions to some of these problems. Additionally, the employees might be asked to also consider how their own role as a part of the environment might facilitate unsafe practices in their fellow employees. This type of focus is perhaps addressed most effectively by those writing about systems thinking.[19] Of vital importance when using this zone, is that employees be given a true sense that they can speak their mind, that their input will be given fair consideration, and that they will not be penalized in any way for providing candid feedback in the first place. Chapter 7 addresses dialogue in workplace learning and the influence of learners' conceptual frameworks and storylines.

Zone 4: Community Approach–Organizational Context. Addressing the community through an organizational context lens is the fourth zone from which workplace interventions can take place. It is similar to Zone 3 in that it focuses on the organizational and systemic, but in this case, not only are the organizational factors taken into account, the specific interventions themselves are directed at the organizational structures of the workplace. The focus in this zone is not the individual, though the individual certainly is a factor in any group, but rather the organizational dynamics that shape a workplace. In the parlance of Illeris' global learning model, this would concentrate more on the interplay of the *social* and the *sociality*, and in his workplace model, the *production* and the *community* aspects of the social dimension.[20]

An example of how an organization would deal with the safety problems we have been discussing using this zone would be to identify all of the core structures and social dynamics of the organization that permit, foster, and in some cases maybe even require unsafe practices, and then "design them out" or at least put in place a series of changes that will, over time, remove or limit their negative effect.

For instance, if the engineering of the package production line requires that stopping the conveyor system jams up the production process, re-engineering the system in a way that permits employees to be able to remove packages without stepping upon to the moving belts would greatly diminish the practice. Perhaps there are bottlenecks, or the machinery is old and frequent jams occur, which require employee intervention. This zone would require looking more at the process, be that poor supervision, micromanagement, or excessive pressing for higher speed and production that may be causing the unsafe practices. Perhaps an overemphasis of Taylorist production methods is causing a problem. Understaffing could also be a cause.

It doesn't take a great deal of thought to realize that this fourth zone could be a touchy one. It would be easier in most cases, and perhaps less painful for management, to simply train the bad behavior out and the good behavior in. Like all the zones, this zone has inherent assumptions at the base of it. Among them are the assumption that changing the organizational structures will serve to modify the individual's behavior in the final analysis, and also the assumption that a great many of the safety problems are the fault of the organizational structures to begin with.

Practical Implications for the Zones

When looking at learning this way, there are several noteworthy implications for learning in general and workplace learning in specific. First, if learning occurs in these four zones and actions can be taken in each of the four zones that will ultimately facilitate learning, then it must follow that all actions taken by managers, supervisors, and trainers in the workplace that touch these fours zones are in themselves teaching acts, whether intended to be or not. *This, by extension, and perhaps more importantly, means that leadership of some sort is occurring all the time through all of these domains of learning.*

This is a daunting idea because it removes intentionality from a great portion of teaching that actually occurs. Professionals are *not* unintentional in their actions and neither are true experts. This is also an area where those who consider themselves leaders in the workplace would be generally familiar with. It would not come as a surprise that what you do is seen by others and carries a message of some sort whether you want it to or not. It is one of the benefits those who see themselves as educators, instructors, and trainers can gain by working to see themselves as leaders as well.

As mentioned earlier and depicted in Figure 6.1, the largest zone of intervention is community learning in the community context. This raises the uncomfortable question of what exactly might be being taught on a day-to-day basis since almost every act, if not every act, taken by administrators in the workplace is a teaching act. This would mean, for instance, that when a policy is drafted, whether its purpose is to address some new dynamic or to react (run from, repeat of, or reach for) to an old dynamic, the writing and implementation of that policy will bring about some sort of change in the social workplace community.

So, the key point here is that while some of the very best opportunities to address problems in the workplace, educationally speaking, come through the ability to address them in the workplace community through the systemic context, a different way of thinking about workplace management is that in real-world experience, *all action is teaching action*. Wenger[21,22] pointed out that this organizational type of learning is the most potent type of learning so it must concern the workplace leader that at all times the learner is being taught through the most powerful of all mediums while the organization's main line of agency through teaching is through meager classroom interventions.

Second, the zones provide a rubric through which workplace management and educators can plan for holistic and effective training programs that have a real-world effect. Addressing learning transfer from all four zones rather than only one or two, is certain to increase efficiency. Furthermore, if each of these areas is a space that some form of teaching takes place, than each of these zones is a place in which learning engagement and motivational immediacy is important.

Leaders who are outside what would be considered the formal instructional side of things at work can see windows of opportunity to influence the culture and behavior of the workplace as a whole by the non-instructional activities that they are busy with most of each day. This is where those who are leaders can increase their reach by seeing themselves as workplace instructors of a powerful type, each time they make any decision at all in their sphere of responsibility.

The third implication is a combination of the first two in that the most effective workplace interventions must include multiple dimensions in which training is facilitated. Newer, more effective, fairer, and more mutually beneficial policies can be implemented by using the four zones, but at the same time, a very close examination of what has been taught unintentionally through the lesser-known zones must be undertaken to locate practices that have "taught" employees to be, as a community, as they presently are. It may be the case that for every action taken, several more actions need to be modified or rescinded (remember that employee learners need to be demotivated at times). Once leadership understands that it is engaged perpetually in teaching acts it will be compelled to attend to ongoing unintended instruction while at the same time planning purposeful counter instruction going forward.

The fourth implication, and the one most closely connected to the concepts addressed in this book, is that if there are four zones of teaching, learning, and leading, there are also four zones of motivational immediacy.

Always Leading, Always Teaching

Thinking over these zones of workplace learning, it should be clear to everyone that one is always teaching someone else no matter what one is doing (or not doing, in fact). Acknowledging this principle leads one invariably to seeing clearly that one is leading and teaching everywhere and always. When faced with these two realities of human learning in the workplace, you have two choices – be overwhelmed and continue as you have been, or see this as a tremendous opportunity to extend the power of your reach as a leader and educator in the workplace. This sort of revelation is akin to finding out that there are entirely new markets that are untapped and which you can move into. Those who want to be doers and get things done with more and more effectiveness, efficiency, and power will, I have no doubt, choose the second.

Notes

1 Taylor, J. E., & McKissack, J. (2014). Zones of intervention: Teaching and learning at all times and at all places. *International Journal of Vocational Education and Technology*, *5*(3), 21–33.
2 Taylor, J. E. (2022). *Motivational immediacy: Fostering engagement in adult learners*. Stylus.
3 Taylor, J. E. (2022). *Motivational immediacy in the workplace: Facilitating learner engagement in training environments*. Routledge.
4 Center for Creative Leadership. www.ccl.org/articles/leading-effectively-articles/what-is-leadership-a-definition/#:~:text=Leadership%20is%20defined%20by%203%20outcomes%20%E2%80%94,never%20achieve%20alone.%20Published%20May%2015%2C%202024
5 Maxwell, J. C. (2022). *The 21 irrefutable laws of leadership: Follow them and people will follow you*. Harper Collins Leadership.

6 Taylor, J. E. (2022). *Motivational immediacy in the workplace: Facilitating learner engagement in training environments.* Routledge.
7 Lave, J., & Wenger, E. (1991). *Situated learning: Legitimate peripheral participation.* University of Cambridge Press.
8 Wenger, E. (1998). *Communities of practice: Learning, meaning, and identity.* Cambridge University Press.
9 Wenger, E. (2000). *Communities of practice: Learning, meaning, and identity* (1st ed.). Cambridge University Press.
10 Lave, J., & Wenger, E. (1991). *Situated learning: Legitimate peripheral participation.* University of Cambridge Press.
11 Wenger, E. (1998). *Communities of practice: Learning, meaning, and identity.* Cambridge University Press.
12 Illeris, K. (2017). *How we learn: Learning and non-learning in school and beyond* (2nd ed.). Routledge.
13 Illeris, K. (2017). *How we learn: Learning and non-learning in school and beyond* (2nd ed.). Routledge.
14 Wenger, E. (1998). *Communities of practice: Learning, meaning, and identity.* Cambridge University Press.
15 Wenger, E. (2000). *Communities of practice: Learning, meaning, and identity* (1st ed.). Cambridge University Press.
16 Dale, M., & Bell, J. (1999). *Informal learning in the workplace. Research brief no. 134.* Department for Education and Employment.
17 Argyris, C., & Schon, D. A. (1996). *Organizational learning II: Theory, method and practice reading.* Addison-Wesley.
18 Lave, J., & Wenger, E. (1991). *Situated learning: Legitimate peripheral participation.* University of Cambridge Press.
19 Senge, P., & Lannon-Kim, C. (1991). Recapturing the spirit of learning through a systems approach. *School Administrator, 48*(9), 9–13.
20 Illeris, K. (2011). *The fundamentals of workplace learning: Understanding how people learn in working life.* Routledge.
21 Wenger, E. (1998). *Communities of practice: Learning, meaning, and identity.* Cambridge University Press.
22 Wenger, E. (2000). *Communities of practice: Learning, meaning, and identity* (1st ed.). Cambridge University Press.

Chapter 7

Conceptual Frameworks, Storyline, and Dialogue

All of the concepts that have been shared in the previous chapters keep leading in the same direction – *the learner's viewpoint is essential.* This chapter will introduce a little of what goes on in the learner's mind in a learning situation and propose some practical keys for tapping into that knowledge in ways that will help you be able to connect better and be more motivationally immediate.

Work within the Storyline

Conceptual Change

A line of scholarship dating back over 50 years has focused on the interpretive frameworks that individual learners (that would be everyone in every context) use to derive meaning from information.[1] Although it grew out of the "philosophy of science" domain, it has had a significantly practical purpose over the past decades – getting a learner to understand something correctly at the outset (conceptually), so that they could draw accurate inferences from it and make good practical decisions regarding output. Although "practical output" was originally and mostly in reference to school children answering questions correctly or working math problems correctly, the work has significant implications for everyday working life. Recently, these ideas, referred to as conceptual change theories (CCTs), or, more specifically, Framework Theories, have been expanded and applied to workplace teaching and learning.[2,3,4,5] Here, as you might guess, they are being expanded into the realm of leadership, since that is one more domain of teaching and learning.

CCT focuses on efforts to foster a change within a learner, regarding the interpretive framework they understand the world through. This, research has shown, is absolutely vital if the learner is going to accurately interpret information about a given phenomenon. That is, we only

DOI: 10.4324/9781003482079-9

understand anything based on the frame of reference we are viewing it from. Unfortunately, we are not always looking through the correct frame, which causes us to put things together incorrectly.

Framework theories are a more focused subset of CCT and provide one of several explanations for how conceptual knowledge affects learning. Simply put, our understanding of the world is a set of concentric frames (Figure 7.1) that start in the most broad sense (i.e., what we believe about reality) and narrow down to include our views about very specific aspects of the context of the situation. Anytime we change the framework – any one of the boxes – all of the meaning within any of the interior boxes changes its meaning also.

The powerful implication for mentoring, leading, and instructing is this – the learner will always interpret everything you say and do, every policy you write or don't write, according to their *own* conceptual frameworks rather than yours. It cannot be said often enough – leading, mentoring, and instructing are *people* skills, not content skills. It is about the someone, not the something. It is about them, not you. You may indeed have a story to tell, and you may indeed have the authority to tell it. But it is always the learner who 'hears' what you have to say, interprets it within their own frameworks, which you often know nothing about, and makes every day practical (or not) decisions in the workplace.

An anecdote that might be helpful here, to make a complicated theory pretty intuitive, is if you can remember a time when someone was trying to describe something to you or, more likely, was telling you a story about something or someone, and you had the wrong idea about who it was being talked about or what the context was within which the dynamics of the story were taking place. As the story unfolded, you continued to put pieces together to create a picture of it in your mind until one of two things happened. Either you exclaimed in shock, something like "Ann got divorced?!" in which case the person telling the story looked at you like you were crazy and said, "no, I am talking about Cathy," or you said something like, "wait, when did Starbucks start selling hamburgers?" to which the other person said something like "who said anything about Starbucks?" This silly back and forth, of course, does little to address the true character of CCT or framework theory, but it does show how in everyday life, when we are thinking about what we are hearing in the wrong frame of reference, we get it all messed up. With a little thought, it is likely that you can think of a more serious and less silly instance where this occurred in your personal life.

When you transfer this idea over to a leading, mentoring, or instructional situation at work, you can imagine the potential for learners to hear something very different from what you are saying because they are interpreting it through a completely different framework than you are. What is simply and truly an attempt to be more efficient with existing resources at the coffee station can easily become "they are going to downsize and get rid of half of us."

To put a more accessible spin on this, the independently developed, but related idea of storyline is helpful.

The Storyline

The concept of storyline here has a very complicated theoretical background but an equally commonsense meaning and application. It is the meaning and application that is important here. Storyline is connected with the academic work of Harre' and Langenhove[6] and is a part of what is called position theory. It is important to note that I am taking the original thinking of Harre' and Langenhove and applying it is a very narrow and specific context, which they may not have intended.

Imagine a scenario where an instructor is standing in a classroom, or leading a virtual training program, believing that their role is one of support, help, and servant–leadership, while everyone else in the classroom is thinking of the class as punishment, and of the instructor as a weapon of the bureaucracy. It is not difficult to understand just how wide the gulf would be in this situation between the instructor and learner. This scenario would be inefficient, at best, and unpleasant and personally harmful at worst. Position theory with its idea of storyline is a very useful tool for developing a lesson plan that will be motivationally immediate and foster engagement and effectual learning on the part of employee learners.

The notion of position is similar in some ways to that of role. Position theory, contrasted with role theory, which originated in sociology refers to much less stable, more short-term and quickly fluctuating statuses as perceived by ourselves and others, although, importantly, how we position ourselves and how others position us are seldom the same. Since teaching is about the other, it is in many ways more important to understand what others are perceiving as your position than what you perceive it to be. While role theory might include the roles we play as parents, leaders, siblings, colleagues, etc., position theory refers to the position we have in any given moment as perceived by those hearing us as we communicate with them. Position theory is largely a communication theory while role theory is not.

Focusing on the aspects of the theory that pertain most directly to motivational immediacy and workplace leading and learning, Figure 7.1 shows the position theory triad in which there exists (a) the speech act itself, (b) the position of the speaker, and (c) the storyline of the communication.[7] Each of these acts upon and is acted back upon by the other two in ways that shape all communication acts, including educative ones.

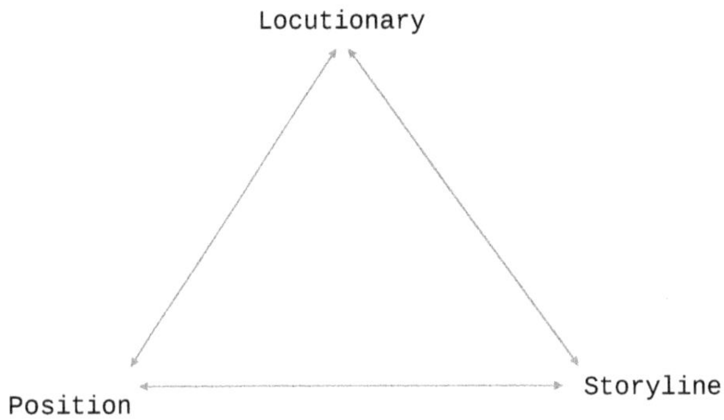

Figure 7.1 Position Theory Triangle.

In Figure 7.1, a triangle is depicted and constructed of three lines with bidirectional arrows indicating cause in both directions. Locutionary acts are at the top, storyline is at the bottom right, and position is at the bottom left.

The speech act (locutionary in Figure 7.1) is subject to variation even without position and storyline, and one can see this by taking a simple sentence and speaking it multiple times while placing the emphasis on a different word each time.

I need you to go to the convenience store.
I ***need*** you to go to the convenience store.
I need ***you*** to go to the convenience store.
I need you to ***go*** to the convenience store.
I need you to go ***to*** the convenience store.
I need you to go to ***the*** convenience store.
I need you to go to the ***convenience*** store.
I need you to go to the convenience ***store***.

The emphasis and inflection placed in each of these words is an example of locutionary dynamics, but the body language that would accompany such statements would also have effect. Saying each of these statements while laughing, frowning, or pointing angrily might change how each of the above sentences is taken. The second to the last one is particularly interesting because even though it is the one on the list that doesn't make clear logical sense, it would communicate cultural sense, most likely be interpreted as some sort of snarky, sarcastic response even if it wasn't. "It is NOT convenient, thank you..."

Position, whether one is trying to position oneself, position others, or is being positioned by others, drastically affects the meaning of the speech act. Take for instance, the following statement: "please stop talking." How would the meaning change if spoken from someone in different positions? How would it be hearable in different ways? Suppose an instructor says it. What about an employee learner? While one can consider instructor and learner to be a more long-term situation that might be better referred to as a role, position is a more powerful conception because even the official instructor in a classroom is always being positioned as the teacher, proud parent, griping employee, or "sold-out" middle management, depending on whether they were sharing technical content, rambling on about their kid's piano recital, complaining about how the IT department is woefully inept, or telling employees what they must do differently in the workplace. The learners will pay different levels of attention depending on the nature of the communication, and the *position* from which it is heard.

Storyline can be understood on a basic level, in accordance with its namesake, known to all of us from very early childhood. We are by nature context-builders. Each person interprets events from within a narrative, which means that every event may have many narratives attached to it. Applying this to teaching and learning, the storyline in position theory refers to the contextual narrative held by the learner, into which the instructor is communicating.

Taking all of this together then, the triangle shown above indicates the interpretive dynamic that the learner is experiencing every time you are trying to communicate anything. Each of the poles on the triangle represents interpretive structures that the hearer is always making in the moment while you are communicating (this works the other direction too), and each one affects and is affected by the others. How you are positioned by the hearer strongly influences what they see the storyline as and how they are hearing and making meaning about what you are saying. The hearer-learner's storyline, in turn, leads to the learner's decision about how to position you, and the locutionary aspects of your speech are interpreted through those two factors while also influencing what the disposition of those two factors actually is. The question arises here, for sure – what does this mean then, for those who wish to make a practical difference in the classroom? It means that the instructor is often teaching specific content without any awareness that the learner is perceiving the entire situation from within a very different storyline than the instructor.

For instance, a communication expert called in to provide customer service training skills to front line workers in a technology firm may think that she is offering a great opportunity for the employees to hone their verbal skills and improve their productivity and job satisfaction. The employees, on the other hand, may think that they are being punished for the company's poor fiscal quarter and that management is bowing to pressure from the Board of Directors and forcing them to sit through the training. The instructor views her own position as a helper, a developmental resource, and a key to enhanced job satisfaction, while the employees are viewing her as "the punisher."

In this case, the disconnect itself is problematic, but the most important viewpoint for how the content is taken in, interpreted, and whether it is internalized and used in the future (transfer) is the employees' viewpoint. Those receiving punishment are not particularly open to guidance and advice, especially from the person issuing the punishment.

Here are examples of two different ways the class could be interpreted and the position that was potentially assigned by the students for each:

Scenario #1
Learner's Storyline
I have worked really hard for years and have not received a pay raise in a very long time. On top of that, I am now being supervised by someone who started after me and doesn't even really know how to do this job. The economy is tanking, the company has made stupid decisions, and now I am being called out as the scapegoat, the problem that needs fixing.

Instructor's Position from <u>the perspective of the learner</u>
Outsider, getting paid lots of money to tell me how to do my job even though they have not done my particular job at this particular company.

Instructor's Communication/Locutionary <u>from the perspective of the learner</u>
Everything said will be interpreted by this position through this storyline.

Scenario #2
Learner Storyline
I am a professional customer service specialist with many years of experience. She is going to use her outside expertise to help me develop strategies for being more successful here. I work hard and do a good job, but I am being rewarded with an opportunity to develop and improve my knowledge and skills. This will help me be more productive, open new opportunities for promotion in the future, and make this job more satisfying.

Teacher Position <u>from the perspective of the learner</u>
Collaborator and subject-matter expert in customer service, consultant, professional equal, and supportive coach.

Communication/Locutionary <u>from the perspective of the learner</u>
Everything said will be interpreted by this position through this storyline.

In each of these two scenarios, the same content is being taught, by the same person, with the same skills, and to the same people with the same skills. But the storyline is quite different between the two and it is easy to see how speech acts might be interpreted very differently in the former than the latter.

The question then, is what to do with this. The theory itself is terribly complicated, but the application is, thankfully, not.

Practical Action

Once again we are faced with theory! So what do we do with it? How should it affect our actions in the workplace? How do we apply this to leading, mentoring, and instructional work within the organization? Here are some concrete practical actions for you to consider.

Know their Storyline – Listening

A simple takeaway here is that you absolutely cannot find out anything at all about the learner's storyline and conceptual framework by talking. It can only be found out by providing space for them to share what it is. This space may be informal, while at the coffee urn, or facilitated through group work in the classroom, carefully designed icebreakers, email correspondence or chat groups in the case of distance learning, or open guided discussions. The hands-down best mode for collecting this information in a meaningful way is to facilitate true dialogue in the classroom as an authentic and important part of the instructional strategy. A dialogue has been considered a conversation without sides,[8] which is an important definition because when one instructs a class there is almost always a "side" being exerted. It is okay to have a side when trying to foster learning, but dialogue is a big part of the process, and for those limited times of dialogue, one's side must be set aside or temporarily suspended in order to really hear the truth.

This is not a "touchy-feely" entreaty, it is a cold, hard clinical fact. If you want to know about the interpretive structures that will ultimately determine what your learners (those following you) are hearing when you talk, then you need to foster periods of true, unfettered, dialogue during which you are willing to set aside your own agenda and make learning from them the only agenda. Once you have learned from them, you are responsible to resume your own agenda. Two things are important to recognize here. First, the learners do realize that you have a job to do and expect you to do it even if they don't like it. Second (and probably more important), you are not really setting your agenda aside when you open the floor to dialogue because opening the floor to dialogue is one of the most necessary and important requirements in order to forward any instructional agenda you may have. If, that is, you are interested in effectual learning and not just some sort of short-term, fake, rote memorization of content details.

How does this fit with the delivery of the content you need to get out? The answer to that question is first to understand that dialogue about the content you have to get out *is* the content you have to get out. If learning is contextually bound and situated in the lived experience of the learners, then the content is contextually bound and situated in the experience of the learners.

A quick practical tip for this is to break what would have been a significant lecture up into a number of very short, 5- to 10-minute mini-lectures, and to surround them with group discussion regarding the information. If you haven't done this before you may be surprised at how on-track, this sort of instruction can remain, despite the group interaction. Key to this process is the instructor's work in advance to prepare for the dialogue and to be able to facilitate successful closure to sessions so that the objectives of the training session come through clearly.

It is natural to fear what sort of crazy thing someone might say during such a session and to be concerned that it will be persuasive for those listening and detract from the points you are needing to make. This is a real risk of this type of collaborative learning but one that can be handled well if one plans in advance and also a risk well worth taking for the positive, long-term results that typically come from it. A simple way to handle this sort of situation, say, when someone points out that the policy isn't good and shouldn't be followed, is to accept the opinion as legitimate, and do the following two things.

First, instead of responding immediately, draw the person out more fully by asking more questions of them about their viewpoint. You can get them to talk about why they feel this way, what circumstances they might think of where they would be right and others where they might be wrong. Asking that person what they think the solution would be, given the policy or method or information being discussed goes a long way toward winning someone over.

Second, following the drawing out of the person making the comment, simply turning to everyone else and saying something like, "well, what do we think? Do we agree, disagree...?" This sounds too simple to be true but many years of experience in this area and a great many professional books on leading dialogue in the workplace will provide evidence that it is often an effective strategy. There will quite often if not always be someone who provides a counter-viewpoint to the one just provided. When you draw them out, you get a firm alternative to the originally expressed opinion, and also a clear segue back to your own structured lesson plans.

I don't doubt that to some this sounds like a good way to unleash chaos in a workplace training situation but that would only be true if one supposed that teaching and learning was simply about conveying clinical content that would be memorized and immediately and permanently adopted by those hearing it. That is not the case, as we have seen, and since effectual learning is what we want and need for long-term learning transfer, allowing the learner to air their thoughts and feelings about the content is the only way to be able to clearly and accurately address any objections that might be out there. Convincing someone of something, as real-world training always is, cannot happen with a lecture and an accompanying slide presentation.

Fostering meaningful discussion is the way forward to understanding the conceptual framework and storyline of the learner. Before moving on to understanding our own storyline, one final word about moving forward with this method safely and responsibly. Prior to beginning a training session, it is a good idea to let those present be aware of the process that will be used, and to take just a few short minutes to get the group to develop together a few behavior rules of conduct for the session. This is a somewhat common practice now and I have done this for many years. In nearly every case, and possibly every case, the rules that were developed by the group were entirely sufficient for the conversation going forward. Seldom will you have to add any missing rules of conduct if you allow this process enough space to fully develop. Still, if you feel like there is a rule that needs to be added, it is okay to put it out there to the group. Again, although you have the right to impose the rule, you will often find that if you have to add one, simply sharing it and asking what the group thinks of it will confirm the rule as a group product (unless you are attempting a very strict and unnecessary rule) rather than a mandate from you.

This is not easy to pull off and definitely lacks the safety and structure of being able to turn your back on everyone, stare at the screen, and click to the next slide. It will require more work and more preparation and more knowledge. It will be difficult, but it will be effective. Expect to make mistakes but understand that a great many people were not actually learning from the more traditional way you were teaching anyway. Training transfer from traditional methods has been so abysmal over the years that you really don't have much to lose in terms of practical efficiency. There is a profound amount to gain.

Know Your Storyline – Reflecting

Since teaching is about connection, and you are the one with specific content that you are charged with sharing, it is not enough to know what the individual storylines are for the learners. You must know what your own storyline is as well. In other words, if you are going to connect with your learners in a way that produces effectual learning, you need to be able to merge storylines in a way where it all makes sense and there is consensus about the way forward. This requires a bit of critical self-reflection. One must ask the following questions along with many others.

What is your *why*? Why are you training, leading, mentoring, and teaching? What drives you in general and what specifically in terms of the specific topic and content you are teaching? Just as the employee learner has an entire scenario (storyline) established in their head about why this training is being given to them, you also have a storyline about the training, the context, the origin of the rules and policies at hand, and the reason the employees need to hear it. Perhaps yours is more accurate because of your position in the organization, or perhaps not, but one thing that is very true is that it is not more or less important than the learners if you want to foster effectual learning – acquisition and acceptance – across the board.

Why is your why? Okay, you are doing well if you can clearly identify why you are doing what you are doing and why it is important. But given that there are so many alternatives, do you know why that is your why? Why is it important to you more than other things? And, potentially, why is this more important to you than many other people? You cannot get anyone to become passionate about something that you are not. That is a basic rule of leadership and teaching alike.

Reconcile the Storyline – Collaborating

Use your knowledge of their storyline to find a way to lead them to your storyline (or change your storyline, or theirs). Despite all of the potential benefits of engaging in this sort of educational effort the purpose of all of this exploration of the self and other is ultimately to facilitate effectual learning of the content by those you are responsible to provide instruction and leadership for. The goal is to use the knowledge you obtain about everyone's storylines to foster authentic learning and acceptance of the content.

Since conceptual change framework theories depict frames, or boxes, I refer to the main process here as "build the box and then fill it." Learning about all of the various boxes out there ensures that all of the content that needs to be shared is being heard in a common framework, an accurate framework, and one that is conducive to seeing the validity of the content to begin with. The only way to an authentic effectual learning space is to make sure you are engaging in an authentic, personal, and safe sharing space. Working to find commonalities between storylines, to build new ones, and to, in some cases, remove faulty, inaccurate ones is the most effective path forward toward authentic learning and long-term training transfer.

Notes

1 Vosniadou, S. (2013). *International handbook of research and conceptual change* (2nd ed.). Routledge.
2 Taylor, J. E. (2022). *Motivational immediacy: Fostering engagement in adult learners.* Stylus.
3 Taylor, J. E. (2022). *Motivational immediacy in the workplace: Facilitating learner engagement in training environments.* Routledge.
4 Frye, S., Taylor, J., & Stafford, A. (2017). The first fifteen minutes: Learning engagement, learning resistance, and the impact of initial teacher-student contact. In C. X. Wang (Ed.), *Theory and practice of adult and higher education* (p. 342). Information Age Publishing Inc.
5 Taylor, J. E., & Frye, S. (2020). "Disillusioned by experience" using conceptual framework theories to understand and mitigate learning resistance in teacher in-service training. *International Journal of Adult Vocational Education and Technology*, *11*(2), 24–39. https://doi.org/10.4018/IJAET.2020040103
6 Harre, R., & Langenhove, L. V. (1999). Introducing positioning theory. In R. Harre, & L. V. Langenhove (Eds.), *Positioning theory* (pp. 14–31). Blackwell.
7 Harre, R., & Langenhove, L. V. (1999). Introducing positioning theory. In R. Harre, & L. V. Langenhove (Eds.), *Positioning theory* (pp. 14–31). Blackwell.
8 Isaacs, W. (1999). *Dialogue and the art of thinking together.* Doubleday.

Chapter 8

Instructional Methods and Lesson Plans

One of the fundamental underlying principles upon which motivational immediacy is based is that educating, training, and leading are all people skills, not content skills. This is another one of those things that leaders tend to intuitively know about leadership, and neither leaders nor trainers seem to know about the instructional side of things. Knowing something is about the *something*, teaching something to someone is about the *someone*. Given that, every one of the principles laid out in this book require and depend on one foundational thing as far as practice goes – the learner (and those who will be led) absolutely must be heard.

The problem is that our training spaces – formal or informal – are designed with the voice of the teacher in mind rather than the student. After all, why would the person there to learn something need to be heard more than the person "with the knowledge?" The answer is that knowing something is about the something and teaching someone is about the someone. It is not a content skill; it is a *people* skill. And, as anyone who is known as having charisma and natural people skills will know, being good with people is about hearing them, not making sure they hear you.

The last chapter laid out some of the reasons why we need to hear from the learners in all cases. And, not just hear surface level, token fragments (i.e., standard ice-breaker exercises). The chapter went on to claim that fostering dialogue in any training session is imperative. A key point was that to teach this way required more work not less. In particular, it requires more planning work before the training session. One of the reasons the idea of leading dialogue can seem so scary is that one can't know what is going to come up during a session and it therefore seems impossible to plan at all.

The acronym provided below lays out a general guideline for thinking through what one is trying to convey in a classroom – what one is trying to foster acquisition *and* acceptance of, and some basic ways to collaborate with the learner to achieve the desired educational goal.

DOI: 10.4324/9781003482079-10

C-O-N-N-E-C-T Through Lesson Plans

Consider your primary objective. Every instructional process you start out on has more than one objective. For instance, we might want employee learners to get to know one another, begin to build a common organizational culture, and become familiar with the policies, procedures, and structures of the workplace. The primary objective would be the one of these objectives that is the most important, if push came to shove, and one of the objectives got in the way of the other. The primary objective is vital in all training situations because there are likely many different objectives, but they are not of equal value and, importantly, often some may contradict others.

In a training class for public transportation rail operator instructors, a debate between instructors developed because certain instructors were requiring bus operators to read publicly in class from a policy and procedure book as part of one of their classes. Several instructors did not like this practice because they said that quite a number of rail operators at their location were not able to read out loud well, particularly in public while nervous, and that to force them to do so was unnecessary and caused them disruptive stress which might ultimately get in the way of their learning. The opposing team, so to speak, felt that reading in public was something that the bus operators would be required to do at some point, and therefore good practice to have them "buck up and learn how to do it" while still in training.

In a situation like this, knowing what the primary objective is for a particular training class session is very important because it will provide the answer for this sort of dilemma. When asked what the primary objective of that training situation was, the instructors answered that the primary objective of that particular training session was for the rail operators to become familiar with all of the basic policies and procedures for their job.

In this scenario, if the primary objective is to learn the policy, to become familiar with it, and to understand what it means, then all instructional decisions must be made in accordance with whatever will advance that objective in the most efficient way. If other secondary goals can be met at the same time without conflicting with or diminishing the primary objective, it is okay to work toward them as well. But in the case of the reading aloud task, reading aloud (for the purpose of teaching them to read aloud) was working in direct conflict with and opposition to the goal of becoming familiar with the policy.

Anyone who has had to read aloud in a group before knows that a couple of things are going on while a few others are decidedly not. First, while everyone else is reading their part, you are counting how many people there are between them and you, and then trying to count out and find which paragraph or section you are going to have to read. Second, you are trying to scan for trouble words and tricky phrases, to sort out any problems before you have to read it. Third, while you are actually reading it, after having not heard what anyone else was reading before you, you are actually so focused on reading the words properly in front of you that you finish without any real idea of what you read. This may be a bit of an exaggeration for some, but near enough for most of us.

In this case, the learning to read aloud objective was not the primary objective and therefore needed to be cut loose. Perhaps it could be the primary objective at another time. Or perhaps it could even be a secondary objective during a class where it would not trip up the primary objective.

Obtain thorough information on learners. If teaching someone is about the someone, then it is absolutely vital to ensure that one is as familiar as possible with each individual learner in the room. Chapter 7 shared the concepts of conceptual frameworks and storylines, and if these two cognitive realities are dictating how information is taken in and encoded, then the only way forward to truly effective teaching is to be able to lay out material in ways that are a good fit for the individual's conceptual framework and storyline. And, of course, the only way to do that is to know what it is. It is important to note here that an individual's storyline could be wildly outside the norm and simply not accurately aligned with what your intentions are as an instructor. The good news is that you needn't simply try to fit your objectives into the sometimes technically inaccurate viewpoint of the learner. A part of addressing the learner's storyline is to change it as part of your instruction (that is at least a part of the point of this chapter). On the other side of the coin, you cannot possibly be effective in changing someone's frame of reference if you have no idea what it is, at least not on purpose.

Finding space to hear from the learner is tough, especially if you have been given a curriculum that is chock full of content that you must transmit to everyone (see Chapter 9). But there are ways to do it. The best possible way is to design your lesson so that it includes a significant amount of dialogue (see Chapter 7). When this is not possible, and, to be fair, it is often not possible given our present training environment, there are other ways to find out about learners. Talking to learners as they come into the classroom before the class is one way. The important thing here is to not see this as some sort of simple social requirement (I am well, how are you?) but as an instructional strategy in which you are learning about who the learner is so that you can work with the learner to find common ground for a shared goal (almost sounds like a leadership style of instructing).

Breaks and lunches are also good opportunities. Again, if you are someone who enjoys hanging out with folks and would never hole up in a corner for your lunch escape to find your center (holing up is my own default move), you need to remember that the point of this is effective instruction, not checking a social box. That doesn't mean, of course, that you shouldn't authentically connect with learners by chatting about everyday (non-course-related) things, but it does mean that you should be getting to know the other so that you can help them learn. That is, after all, the only reason they are spending time with you anyway. Beyond this, there are many ways to make reasonable inferences and predictions based on prior interactions with employees in similar situations and reasonable attempts at empathy.

Navigate with empathy. Empathy is a keyword here, not sympathy. Sympathy may help as well, but it is not entirely necessary. The difference matters. While empathy understands what others are going through, sympathy feels bad for them. Sympathy likely will make you a better instructor, but empathy is required to be good at all.

Empathy is what will help an instructor arrive at a reasonably inferred idea of what the learner's storyline is for the training, along with other motivational factors that play a major role. Empathy is what will help one with the next step below, but before moving on, it is probably worth addressing an objection that is sometimes raised on this point. Empathy, of course, is a key skill in leadership as well and long understood by strong leaders to be vital.

If drawing such conclusions about employee learners before even starting a class seems a bit off, that is because the best way to do it is to gather such information all along the way from everyone around you so that you know what is going on before you sign off on some new training effort to begin with. However, even if you do this, you will still need to fill in the blanks to the best of your ability in an effort to help foster the best learning environment you can. After all, in our personal lives, it would be offensive if we didn't try our best to please the other even when we were not told every little thing that they wanted or expected. In most human social interactions, we do expect others to make an effort to understand to the best of their ability what we might feel, think, and like, and the leading and teaching process is no different.

On the other hand, we certainly need to be open to the reality that we may be wrong. Being open to our own potential for errors is also a part of being a good instructor. So yes, making some reasonable predictions about what your learners might be thinking and feeling will make you a better teacher – if you make plans accordingly. And, as things move forward, you will be listening very closely to all sorts of different cues your learners will give you and in the event you are wrong, and you often will be, you will be able to adjust on the fly because you will have motivational immediacy at the very front of your mind the whole time you are teaching.

Note all potential resistance. This step is the culmination of the empathy step and "obtain thorough information from the learner" step. Given all of the information you have either gleaned or inferred to the best of your ability, you consider all of the possible reasons that any one of your learners might actually be motivated to ignore you, tune you out, disagree with you, and determine in their mind that they will never be doing that thing you have suggested in class. Why would they possibly be motivated to *not* learn?

Working with motivational fields, not factors, you can begin to think through, in advance, what that field may look like given all of the information you have on hand at the time. Additionally, you can be very familiar with all of the main categories and reasons that learners both reasonably and unreasonably resist learning and may be motivated to not engage.

Why would a good instructor engage in such a negative task? The answer to this question is easy, really. The good instructor will engage in this because it is a deeply learner-centered approach and is not negative at all. The expert instructor seeks to listen and understand the learner's point of view. They seek to connect with the learner where they are and to make the journey from there. They acknowledge that human motivation is not binary and goes with equal energy in either direction with regard to learning. As a professional, you are aware that your learner may in fact be motivated to *not* learn. In order to demotivate such learners to not learn and, in turn, motivate them to learn (often two different steps, but sometimes the same), you simply must be aware of what their motivations might likely, or even possibly be. This is a part of working with the motivational field of the learner. For example:

- The learner may think they already know all there is to know about their job.
- The learner might think they know more than the instructor about how to do their job.
- The learner might believe that they are being unfairly punished for something outside of their control, such as a bad fiscal quarter or atypically difficult customers.
- The learner might believe that the instructor's "theory" is not applicable to practice.
- The learner might believe that instructors (and management) are out of touch with the day-to-day operations.

These factors and others may be in play during the class and making an attempt to catalogue them in advance will prepare the instructor to connect more easily, quickly, and effectively to the learner, address those concerns, and get past them.

Engineer all content to preemptively address resistance. Taking all of the reasons above that a given group of learners may be motivated to resist rather than engage, the very basic, important, but often overlooked step, is to add responses to each and every one of these directly into the lesson plan, *as part of the content,* and use them to slowly but surely bring each learner to a place where their resistance has dropped and they are engaged with the content, with their classmates, and with you as the instructor. *In practice, the five concerns listed above will now become an authentic and irreplaceable part of the training content itself.*

The Learner May Think They Already Know All There is to Know About Their Job

For the first half of my career as an educator, I responded to this (at least in my head) with "no, you don't know all there is to know about your job." That, of course, was to be followed with the evidence that there was more to know, the importance of knowing it, and the efficacy and accuracy of the information I was getting ready to unload. These days, I am more likely to respond with a genuine question – "why do think you know all there is about your job?" At some point, I am going to share the new information, but taking a few minutes to explore the learner's viewpoint will help me be more effective in doing so.

Taking the time to dialogue with the learner as part of your lesson is the fastest way to have them accept the content you might share with them. This awareness may be facilitated by group discussions in which members work together to find difficult workplace problems that they have experienced and a related set of questions, or by sharing a case study that involves an ill-defined problem and then having a class discussion to expose weak areas.

Importantly, the training content now must have the employee learner's blind spots or knowledge and skill limitations built into the list of learning objectives. Whatever the actual method that is used, motivationally immediate training requires that *these steps and the related purposes be considered a part of the content, not merely some preparatory exercise leading up to it.* The practical purpose of seeing it as part of the content is that a failure to do so – to see it only as a pre-content exercise – leads far too often to it getting cut when time is short.

The Learner Might Think They Know More Than the Instructor about How to Do Their Job

First, do they? They might. In fact, often they do. That is because those who are teaching in some sort of full-time capacity are naturally spending less time on the job doing the job. The good news is that we can stop being defensive about this, if we properly understand what teaching is. For this, it is important to go back to leadership for a minute. No one seems to mind that the most significant leaders in all of history, including the ones we are following every day of our normal lives, never seem to know the details about how to do *anything*! The greatest professional leaders typically have a string of hardworking, detail-attentive, highly competent professionals attending to details, implementing projects, setting up programs and organizations, and manufacturing products.

Why then, do we follow leaders? We follow leaders because they do, in fact, have information we need in order to be the best that we are able to be and to produce within our highest capacity. They have vision and know how to convey it to us, or, more accurately to instill it within us. One might ask why we are willing to follow leaders who know less than us about our immediate domains of experience, but not instructors who suffer from the same limitation. The answer to this is simple, but not intuitive. Effective leaders lead us by making sure we are aware that they think we know our stuff, are highly capable, and can exceed our own expectations. When they do this, we lean in to listen. We want to hear all they have to say and hope we miss nothing.

Instructors, on the other hand, take the learners' ignorance as the point of origin, the ground-zero for the instructional action. And, given the way we have all come to understand teaching and learning, this makes all the sense in the world to us. Except it isn't true, and it doesn't actually work very well. Instructors most certainly need to establish credibility, but not the kind that is usually sought. Instructors are leaders in the learning world, they are facilitators of individual growth and development, and they are the vision castors for what the workplace could be like if we all worked together to expand our capacity or knowledge.

That last sentence is a pretty strong one and might need a little support here. In reading it, it would be easy to take issue with the capacity expansion part especially because we tend to think of capacity as a fixed state of our ultimate or maximum unreached capabilities rather than our *present* maximum capacity, given our present mental, physical, psychological, philosophical, social, and motivational states. Words can carry whatever meaning we wish to ascribe to them but seeing capacity as fixed with regard to learning is a mistake because it assumes that the best sort of instructional work fills one to the edges of this capacity. In reality, the best sort of leadership expands the capacity of the individual so that they can become more than they could have come before, and, likewise, the best instructional work expands the capacity of the learner so that they can learn far more than they could have before your time with them. Danish educational psychologist Knud Illeris actually defines learning as, "any process that in living organisms leads to permanent capacity change and which is not solely due to maturation or aging."[1]

The action item here then, is to avoid trying to argue with learners about whether you know more than them in their particular areas, instead focusing on conveying through multiple means, that you intend to help them increase their capacity to grow and learn and increase their skill in a particular area. Once more, dialogue and collaboration with the learner is the way to proceed with this and during that process, all of the things you do happen to know that they don't will come out loudly and clearly. You won't have to make the case for it because they will be listening for it to begin with. You are a leader and almost everyone wants to listen to a true leader in the end. After all, we typically call someone a great leader mainly because there are many people following them. We may then circle back and try to find out what they have done right, but it is the group running along behind them, hanging on their every word that causes us to designate them as leaders to begin with.

The Learner Might Believe That They Are Being Unfairly Punished for Something Outside of Their Control, Such as a Bad Fiscal Quarter or Atypically Difficult Customers

Thinking back to what the research on conceptual frameworks (Chapter 7) has revealed about how humans learn, every bit of training content is heard, interpreted, made sense of, encoded, and loaded for future use (or not) within a conceptual framework that already exists in the learner's mind. If you don't "build the box" before you fill it, the learned content is very likely to not look anything like it does in the box you are teaching it from information on position theory and the storyline learner's hear training content through.

The Learner Might Believe That the Instructor's "Theory" Is Not Applicable to Practice

This is a simple one, although it seems supremely difficult to pull off in practice. No theory should ever be taught without a relevant application and to do so is to do both the learner and the theory an injustice. The trick here, like in most other areas, is less about coming up with great ways to teach this and more about finding ways to foster conditions in which learners discover it. Use discussion and group exercises to develop the connections. Something as simple (and perhaps silly) as having a competition between groups of employee learners to develop a scenario for which the theory would apply and a true workplace anecdote to make the point. Most of the time, the employees are going to have more knowledge and skill in this area than the instructor does. And, even if they don't, they will find their own experiences more meaningful and valid then they will the instructors.

The Learner Might Believe That Instructors (and Management) Are Out of Touch with the Day-to-Day Operations

First question – are you? It is very likely that you are. This is especially true if you are spending your time building lesson plans while everyone you are going to teach is out building air conditioners. However, leaders hear from the people they lead, and so if you spend a portion of your time in each instructional session working to gather information from the learner *as a part of your content*, and really listening to what their world is like, you will very quickly bridge this gap and know a great deal that you didn't know before. On top of that, the great news about this one is that if the instructor uses group facilitation heavily in the training, carefully creating circumstances through which learners come to the conclusions they need to and weaving in expertise and the requisite technical knowledge where natural gaps occur, the learners won't be much concerned about the instructor's credibility in the first place. They will be busy thinking they had all of the answers, even though it was the instructor who expertly led them there. *Training is not about the teacher knowing the content; it is about the learner coming to know the content.* Whatever is the very most efficient way to do this is, well, the very most efficient way to do this.

An essential part of this entire process, and one that makes it very different from most others written about in instructional training books, is that these processes are considered to be a part of the content, rather than other things that one has to do to prepare the learner. In the real world (and that is the one that most likely has you interested in reading this book), the things you do and the things you teach are one interwoven thing. Remember, what one actually learns from you is what you actually taught.

Connect to your learners in situ. This step is easy for some and tremendously difficult for others. Motivational immediacy is immediate. That means that the effective instructor must be immediate to the individual learners at all points during the class. Faces must be read, body language must be interpreted, and responses must be assessed and clarified. This may sound daunting to some, and it can be challenging, but this is why motivational immediacy is more about changing the way we think, than about any particular practice. The moment one really accepts that teaching is about working with people, knowing people, understanding people, and communicating with people, it becomes a natural step to stay in touch with each and every learner the entire time one is teaching. Teaching is about leading.

Talk to your learners. This step should be easy but isn't for many of us. Small talk is required, icebreakers may be expected, but authentic inquiry into the lives, minds, and especially "hearts" of our learners is a difficult proposition. I have spent nearly 20 years now asking different groups of people to (a) share who their favorite teacher was from their entire life, from birth to the present time at any level and form of education, and (b) explain why. In all of the years, I have been asking the question a few things have been true 100% of the time. First, in every single case, the person remembers the name of the teacher, no matter how far back the experience was. Sixty-five-year-olds remember the name of their third-grade teacher (Ms. Jones) from that town they only lived in for one school year. Second, in absolutely no cases was the reason that the teacher knew a lot about their subject area. Discussion reveals that this is not because that isn't important, just expected and assumed. In every single case, it was a teacher who connected with them individually, as a human being, met them where they were, and walked some sort of a journey with them. And, it is accurate to say, they are still walking the journey with them all of these years later, even if unaware.

Cognitive, Affective Social (CAS) Worksheet

The worksheet depicted in Figure 8.1 is designed to be used by both instructors and employee learners alike.[2] The instructor should use the worksheet before each training session, and with each significant content point within a lesson. The learners should be given the opportunity to use the worksheet during class, when possible, for two reasons. First, it will help them experience effectual learning (acquisition and acceptance), and second, because they will typically be much better at this than the instructor, especially if they have been on the job for any significant amount of time.

The worksheet takes into account a number of different things. First, it takes into account the three dimensions of learning described by Illeris. The

Learning Dimension	*Classroom*	*Field*	*Effect of F on C*	*Effect of C on F*
Cognitive				
Social				
Affective				

Figure 8.1 The CAS Worksheet.

terms used – cognitive, social, and affective[3] – have been changed by Illeris in his later work,[4] but I have retained them because I think they are clearer, in terms of their application to practice.

Second, the worksheet takes into account the effect that the classroom discussions will have in the workplace, which I have labeled "the field." When practical issues are discussed in the classroom, and the instructor is providing a comprehensive package of content to the employee learner, that "learning" is not static and isolated in a vacuum. It will have to intersect with all of the fluid and constantly changing dynamics of the workplace. For instance, when an electrician apprentice is told quite firmly not to ever use his lineman's tool as a hammer, it will have a very clear and present effect on the job the next day when the foreman and the other six electricians on the jobsite tell him to "shut up and use the tool" to knock that plate off.

Third, the worksheet takes into account the effect that actual experience in the workplace has on the classroom. In the workplace training room, it is very common for the learners to have logged hundreds if not thousands of hours in actual workplace activity. That puts technical and often "canned" training knowledge to a true test and one for which it is very often ill-prepared. An employee who has been reamed out by her more senior co-workers for kicking the brick out of the external door that was propped open for a smoke break at 2 am will smile at your very serious (but in her mind, trivial) line 5, slide 26 mandate to "never prop an external door open for security reasons." The employee absolutely will prop the door open again (read, zero transfer), and ironically, she will do so *especially* because it will ensure her personal security.

In Practice

For the sake of providing a concrete example, consider the case of the lineman's tool. More accurately, it should be called lineman's pliers. More accurate still, it should be referred to as electrician's pliers, but no matter – each trade has its oddities. Lineman's pliers are, well, pliers. But they are used on the jobsite so frequently and for so many things that if one hangs out with electricians for only a short while, honorable mention of one sort or another will come up. Simply put (and for electricians, I am trying to make a point and apologize for any minor inaccuracies), electricians have learned over the years, in the school of "hard knocks" probably, that these pilers are robust enough that they can be used, in a pinch, as a stand-in for a hammer. Hammering, however, even with a hammer, takes its toll over time. When the hammering is conducted by something that was not designed to be a hammer, the vitality of the something is greatly diminished. It takes little imagination to understand that the thing being hammered might also suffer an indignity or two when being struck by something that was not designed for that purpose. Because of this potential damage, by both the tool and the recipient of the hammer alike, it is a routine part of apprentice training to be told to not, under any circumstances, use the lineman's tool as a hammer.

Cognitive

It is a gross oversimplification to split these three dimensions apart because they all interact with one another, and there is a cognitive context to both the social and emotional. However, for the sake of practical use, the cognitive dimension refers to the more clearly recognizable aspects of cognition and learning concepts and skills. This category would include all of the train-the-trainer information related to human skill acquisition (e.g., primacy–recency, cognitive load, etc.).

The cognitive part of the learning task is the easy part, relatively speaking. It is the most controllable, most stable, and least robust to change. It is strange then, that this is the dimension of learning that the training profession nearly obsesses about. It may actually be natural to focus on this area especially because it is controllable, relatively stable, and robust to change, but if we do so we are, in essence, ignoring the dimensions that require the most effort and focus if we wish for success. Experts don't take the easy route if it is much less effective.

Using the example of the lineman's pliers, it is easy to see that the more straight-forward part of the training process would include sharing the proper information with the learners – that they are not to use the tool as a hammer (or any number of various other purposes) – and to perhaps share why that is the case. There may be more here, but for the sake of clarity, and because this is the one area of workplace training that is reasonably effective, I will leave it at this.

Social

The social is where the learning process starts to become complicated and where the training process begins to become halting at best and completely unsuccessful at worst. The social dimension has everything to do with the peer work dynamics while on the job. For every workplace, there is a general culture of both community and of the work task itself (Illeris refers to this as production in his model, 2017). Each of these exerts tremendous pressure on employee learners to come into compliance with those cultural practices in the workplace.

Although this is empirically well-grounded,[5,6,7] it is anecdotally obvious as well. A large share of the training content is often related to changing a number of different, entrenched practices in the workplace. There is the way employees are taught to do things and "the way we do it out here." Going back to the notion of the employee not engaging because the new learning contradicts the old,[8] it is not that employees don't want to learn from training, just that they have already learned too well in the workplace.

In the lineman's plier situation, apprentices will readily share how they are expected to use the tool anyway they are asked to use it, and to do it quickly without offering up their "two cents." While there are some job sites that have more by-the-book supervisors, most often, the apprentice is working with a seasoned professional in the trade, and in these instances, most will admit that there is no way they are going to buck the system out there "where it matters." And, if a professional trainer is fair, they will admit that the apprentices have a good point.

In this case, the power of the social will outrun the cognitive nearly every time. When working through this worksheet then, before a class, it becomes immediately obvious that simply transmitting factual knowledge and expectations to the employees will be woefully ineffective. If the instructor is working for effectual learning (acquisition and acceptance), then two things are clear. First, something has to be done out in the workplace to shift this practice (see zones of intervention in Chapter 6). Second, if one has any hope of actually swaying the opinion of a learner strongly enough to make that learner resistant to the powerful peer pressure on the job site, then the instructor must be motivationally immediate.

It may not be 100% effective, but if there is any hope of changing this behavior, it will require a very frank conversation among the employee learners in the classroom, and the instructor absolutely must provide a safe space for honesty. Discussions need to be facilitated around these dynamics in the workplace without the learners being penalized for admitting their jobsite transgressions related to the tool use, without it getting back to their foreman that they have been open about these things, and without it being held against them in the future. Having authentic conversations about these practices may not fully change them, at least immediately, but there is no hope of doing so without them. As per usual, PowerPoint slide number six, with the little verbal diatribe attached, is not going to cut it. It is a waste of time.

Affective

It is in this affective domain that the other two meet and produce something difficult to control and predict. Not only do emotions regarding the content and job itself affect the learning choices of the employee, but all manner of incidental emotions that have little to do with the workplace, coworkers, or the training content at hand. Studies have shown that incidental anger (anger that was not related to the situation at hand) resulted in study participants being less willing to take advice from others.[9] Again, providing space for the learner to share their own conceptual frameworks, their own storylines, and their own experiences, opinions, and yes, feelings, is the only way forward to getting very complicated human beings to change the way they see any aspect of the world enough to transfer it to long-term practice in the workplace.

Effect of Field on Class

The question here, for the instructor first and then for the instructor to draw from the learner, is "what is the effect of that job site dynamic on the employee as they are sitting in your classroom hearing you talk about how to use the lineman's tool?" And, an easy further step, "what would you do in their place?" (empathy). Simply thinking through this should provide some insight into how to make the point more powerfully with the learner. Likewise, facilitating a discussion with the employee learners themselves about this dynamic, how it affects them, etc., will greatly improve the chances that they will change their behavior on the jobsite, although it will certainly stop short of guaranteeing it.

Effect of Class on Field

Finally, there is the consideration of what the effect of the classroom discussions will be in the field, on the jobsite. This one may seem silly, given that the whole point of the training is to have the person end up doing what you are teaching them to do in the class. However, as all training professionals know, this is sadly, just not always the case. There are many ways that training in the classroom can end up playing out on the job and in order to predict it at all well, and adjust for it in advance is to plan for all of the contextual elements of the jobsite.

For instance, the employee learners, if they have been on the jobsite before, can share with you that, in the case of the lineman's tool, the apprentice is going to be told to shut up and do what they are told. And, if they share that it was how they were taught in the classroom, they are going to be told another few things that I will leave out here. If this is a reality of the work, and if it can't be controlled, then it is disingenuous to not discuss it with the learners and plan accordingly. To fail to do so (slide 6, line 4) is to risk having your learners lose respect for the training (and other training courses down the road – remember conceptual framework development). Further, it makes for inert training that is more of a checked-box, than a learning experience for the employee.

Putting the Pieces Together

In this case, the situation seems somewhat hopeless, but at least by talking it through *with* the employee learners, rather than talking *at* them, there is the possibility of first, working out a strategy together for using the tool properly. Using the worksheet to think through these sorts of dynamics with each topic in the lesson is hard. Doing so, however, will provide a great deal of information about the true context you are speaking into, help you learn more about the learners in your classroom, and provide ways to potentially navigate situations in ways that the learner may, at least in the long-run, end up doing the right thing, and encouraging those around them to as well.

Building this type of lesson plan results in a strikingly different product than the use of a traditional content-based lesson plan. But that is the difference – traditional planning tools are typically content-based and what I am proposing here is deeply learner-based. It is because of this that when you place the two side by side the former will seem very neat and technically clear, while the latter will be infused with all kinds of nuance and messiness. This returns us to the whole notion of remembering what human learning is in its natural state. Human learning is naturally messy because we are naturally messy. It is one of the things that makes us beautifully creative and diverse. It is one of the reasons we can create so many awful problems in the world but also why we can so often come up with really great ways to solve them.

Human learning is not in a scientific outline and teaching can't be either. Leaders in the workplace tend to know this, but think it doesn't apply to instructional acts. Instructors in the workplace tend to not know this at all, or at least, be fearful of what might happen if we took the cap off and let it out in our workplace learning spaces. It will take courage to apply any of these principles and to use any of these methods. It is just the sort of thing those passionate about becoming even better at what they do would take a crack at.

Notes

1 Illeris, K. (2017). *How we learn: Learning and non-learning in school and beyond* (2nd ed.). Routledge.
2 Taylor, J. E. (2022). *Motivational immediacy in the workplace: Facilitating learner engagement in training environments.* New York: Routledge.
3 Illeris, K. (2007). *How we learn: Learning and non-learning in school and beyond.* Routledge.
4 Taylor, J. E. (2022). *Motivational immediacy in the workplace: Facilitating learner engagement in training environments.* Routledge.

5 Illeris, K. (2017). *How we learn: Learning and non-learning in school and beyond* (2nd ed.). Routledge.
6 Illeris, K. (2011). *The fundamentals of workplace learning: Understanding how people learn in working life*. Routledge.
7 Wenger, E. (2000). *Communities of practice: Learning, meaning, and identity* (1st ed.). Cambridge University Press.
8 Salaman, G., & Butler, J. (1990). Why managers won't learn. *Management Education and Development, 21*, 183–191.
9 Gino, F., & Schweitzer, M. (2008). Blinded by anger or feeling the love: How emotions influence advice taking. *Journal of Applied Psychology, 93*(5), 1165–1173.

Chapter 9

Curriculum and Instructional Design

A Warning about Heresy

It is probably right to alert you to the fact that much of what I am going to write in this chapter is considered heretical by those who are experts in the field of curriculum development. I am comfortable with those experts thinking this because they are right about the heresy part, and also because they are wrong about the curriculum part. It would be unfair if I didn't point out that I am not very good at many of the technical aspects of curriculum development and rely heavily on those who are, in my everyday work. Curriculum experts are right about a great many things, but they are, unfortunately, most often practicing their trade on a piece of ice shelf broken off from the mainland, floating in a massive ocean trying to describe where they are. This is a result of a problem with the educational system, not the curriculum experts per se, and what I am going to share here can have the effect of making them better at what they are already good at. It could also help many of us become better at what we are bad at, which is also important and oftentimes has a greater margin of payoff. If you are reading this as a curriculum designer, you will hopefully see through a little of my hubris here and realize that my hope is to inspire reflection and thought in some of the more entrenched areas of the profession rather than offense to any particular practitioner.

The term heresy I am using here was given my work by a friend and colleague who worked as a professional curriculum development specialist for a state government in the U.S. and came along as a result of my request for feedback. I share this at the outset because it is important to note that what you are going to read here in relation to motivational immediacy and effectual learning, is not in alignment with what you will read in most curriculum manuals you will find on the market. I will do my best to explain why and provide a way to use the principles in this book to continue professional growth in this area.

DOI: 10.4324/9781003482079-11

Some Hazards of Professional Curriculum

There are a number of what might be considered occupational hazards for the professional curriculum profession. These hazards run counter to the implications of what we know about human motivation, human learning, and therefore also training in the workplace. Some of these may be unavoidable in certain situations and it is important to take the constraints of real life into account when providing critiques and making suggestions. However, the downside risks of these practices need to be understood because they are not always necessary in the first place, and also because when they are necessary the hazards can be mitigated at least to a certain degree. Each of these will be laid out below with a few suggestions for how to correct for some of their inherent weaknesses.

Professional Curriculum Development

In terms of motivational immediacy and effectual learning, there has likely been no development more damaging than the emergence of the professional field of curriculum development or instructional systems design (ISD). Somewhere along the line, those who develop curriculum and those who teach curriculum have divided into two separate groups, each with its own set of standards, culture, and even advanced degrees. The problem is not with the curriculum expert, but with the system of having developed even further into those who know stuff, those who organize stuff for others to teach, and those who teach stuff divided into three groups. Simply put, curriculum and ISD are fields of practice that tend to elevate and focus upon content rather than the learner.

A few weaknesses of this system are the development of rigid rules for curriculum design that are out of touch with established (and newly discovered) learning concepts, professionals who are developing curriculum but never teaching it, content-driven curriculum intended to be used for what is actually a person-driven phenomenon, and the mass production of what is always (no matter on what scale it is rolled out) an organic, grassroots activity.

Content-Driven Curriculum

When curriculum production becomes a profession and trade of its own, then ultimately you have a group writing it who are not ever going to teach it, may not have ever taught it in the past, and in some extreme cases, might not have never taught at all. When subject matter experts (SMEs) constitute a third group, curriculum designers may also be divorced even from any close knowledge of the content, leaving them experts only at constructing curriculum itself. This is allowed to happen and can even happen quite naturally specifically because the narrow division of the teaching and learning process has become its own profession rather than remaining as an integrated whole of the learning-knowledge, teaching-knowledge, and curriculum design triad.

Going back to the work of Illeris discussed in Chapter 6, all human learning includes multiple dimensions and dynamics including cognition, emotion, incentive, volition, environmental effects, societal effects, etc.[1] Learning cannot be broken down into small rigid fragments because people cannot be broken down into small rigid fragments. And since learning can't be broken down in this reductionist way, to do so with curriculum creates a schism between the content and the learner that cannot be easily bridged. Teaching and training are people skills, not content skills. They are people skills because learning is only and always about the learner, and any competent instructor must focus on ways to reach the individual learner. Again, getting someone to "get" something is about the someone. Curriculum design typically has a completely different focus – how best to arrange, manage, and organize content. It may seem like common sense that these activities are done so for the learner, but they are in the truest sense created for the integrity of the content first, and the ease of the teacher second. Both of these things are important, but for the individual learner to be the third runner-up in terms of concern is to miss the point of the entire game. There is an easy-to-see gulf between the concerns of the curriculum designer and the concerns of the classroom instructor, but their concerns should ultimately and mostly be the same.

Curriculum in a Box

The culmination of mass-produced curriculum ends up being curriculum that is "packaged" to be taught by almost anyone. That is, the instructor no longer has to be a subject matter expert (SME) because the curriculum designer or some third person was (see how all of this is developing into a non-human clinical activity?). Now there is a situation where any person can take the curriculum out of the box and teach it because it is self-contained and has all of the learning objectives (however cold and stiff they are), all of the talking points, all of the activities, and all of the assessment items. When examining this entire curriculum process over and against what we know about the organic, messy, human learning process, there is an utter disconnect between the two. Human learning is not a process that can be subjected to Taylorism and put in a factory. That is just what we have done and it is not working at all well.

Here is where the special knowledge of the leader comes into such powerful play. Anyone who is a successful leader is intuitively aware that leading is a deeply organic, person-to-person process that requires both science and art form. If asked to mentor someone on leadership, a formally constructed, enumerated curriculum would not be handed over in a box. There would likely be a significant personal investment and hands-on teaching–learning process. If the mentoring leader did put together a written curriculum of sorts, it would be discussed and massaged into real-world practice under the close supervision of that leader, not a random instructor from the instructor pool. That is, no leader intending to mentor someone in a meaningful way would trust the curriculum to effectively guide an instructor who didn't write it.

Going further, if one is to consider all of the books written on leadership skills and practice to be a form of curriculum, that is a reasonable assessment. However, if that is the case, take a good look at the books written and all of those considered powerful ones are written not in a cold, clinical, scientific sort of way, but in a warm, moving, persuasive way that makes them something akin to motivational speeches, not lectures in biology. There is a reason for this – personal, motivating connection with a specific human being is always in mind. This is largely absent in large-scale, segmented curriculum design in the workplace, where professionals are often hired only to construct technical curriculums because they know something about something rather than something about someone.

The Measurement Fraud

A student of Thorndike, William McCall, is credited with the well-known and often quoted "whatever exists at all, exists in some amount and can be measured."[2] This statement is similar to many others like it that make a great deal more sense in theory than in practice. The history of science portrays a nearly endless line of existing phenomena that were first suspected, then verified by a newfound ability to measure them. Very little effort is made to explain away their presence during the time prior to their successful measure.

The logic of the way we have applied the statement is problematic also. It is a non-sequitur in that it doesn't follow that because something must exist in a quantitative amount, that one would, at any point, have the capacity or skill necessary to measure it. It is a statement about ultimate reality, an ontological proposition, not a practical application. I might tell you that if we can put a man on moon, we could put a person on Mars, and indeed, it might be technically true, but not practically true for some time yet. The statement says something, it just doesn't say anything important about the topic at hand.

The problem is not, of course, with the idea that one should measure learning outcomes where possible. The purposes of this sort of activity are easy to see and include being able to know that one has accomplished the goal one set out to accomplish; knowing what areas need additional focus; and knowing how effective or efficient certain methods are. The mistake is confusing a nuanced utility with an absolute mandate; a useful tool with a meaningful outcome.

We have, in essence, come to value the method of construction more than the usefulness of the structure. Jacques Maritain, a French philosopher writing in the early 1900s, spoke to this when he referred to the "surprising weakness" of education at the time of his writing proceeded from "our attachment to the very perfection of our modern educational means and methods and our failure to bend them toward the end"[3] (p. 3). He also referred to a "cult of the means" that resulted in the "psychological worship" of the means rather than the ends they should be employed to serve (p. 14).

Particularly with curriculum design and ISD, there is a general rule of making sure to have at least one assessment item for each learning objective stated.[4,5] The mandate for this sort of thing is often dressed up and called things like "table of test item specifications" but effectively refers to the need to have alignment.

This makes sense on the surface of it and, in truth, it looks really squared away when each assessment item has a learning objective number parked next to it (e.g., 1.2.a). But it also necessitates that no learning objectives be permitted in the curriculum *unless* they are represented in the assessment list. It follows then, that nothing can be taught, unless it can be measured. That, I will frankly say (and own) is a complete and utter disaster for meaningful education. As already discussed, the emotive, feeling side of learning, the deep personal connection required for motivational immediacy and effectual learning (like leadership), cannot be measured very well or with much accuracy. If a delivery employee is asked on a test "is it okay to text while driving sometime?" every employee who has enough common sense to get and hold a job will say "of course not." That, as we all know, does not match up at all with what is happening on the roadways.

For such a prolific problem, the nature of it is quite simple. The curriculum design process, by a preponderance of the literature, promotes the creation of well-defined learning objectives, the clear connection of objectives to specific assessment measures, and the evidence of curricular and instructional effectiveness via that observable behavior of students. These sorts of rules are a natural progression of formalizing a profession of curriculum itself, detached from teaching and learning, and – like the American Colonial Army that dropped its highly successful methods the moment it started thinking of itself as a "real" army and stood up in straight rows on open ground to be shot at close range – it is natural for it to concern itself with its own professional practice at the expense of the efficacy of its end goal.

This chain of expectations, when coupled with the extreme difficulty and impracticable nature of evaluating effectual learning, creates a situation in which no matter what lip-service is paid to addressing the affective elements in curriculum design, the practice of curriculum design will quietly step around the affective. In essence, although it may not be said exactly this way, the call is to teach only what you can measure.

And this is the essence of the problem. It is one thing to agree that one should always try, to the best of one's ability, to measure something you are trying to achieve, but it is quite another to say that one should never teach anything that is *not* measurable. To agree with this sentiment is to buy-in to a sort of ontological reductionism that badly damages the underlying reality and purpose of learning.

There are a few noteworthy exceptions out there, but they are noticeable in that they are exceptions. Rosemary Caffarella, and Adult Education Scholar, provides the following guidance in her program planning book – "...in constructing program objectives, it is important to state both measurable and nonmeasurable goals."[6]

A final word about measurement concerns the popular, but nefarious S.M.A.R.T. objectives construct.

S.M.A.R.T. objectives have been regularly associated with the ideas of Peter Drucker, namely, his Management by Objectives concept,[7] but was actually first introduced in 1981 by George Doran.[8] The acronym is represented in the following way:

Specific – target a specific area for improvement.
Measurable – quantify or at least suggest an indicator of progress.
Assignable – specify who will do it.
Realistic – ensure it is realistic given present resources.
Time-Related – specify when results can realistically be achieved, given available resources.

It is interesting that Doran immediately follows these criteria with the following words, "Notice that these criteria don't say that all objectives must be quantified on all levels of management. In certain situations, it is not realistic to attempt quantification..." That right there is useful, meaningful and, well, beautiful. This particular line has, unfortunately, I think, not followed along with the criteria itself as it has been employed across domains. When this concept shifted into curriculum design textbooks in the training and development fields, the admonition was stripped of its moderate parameters and delimiting words of caution.

Going even further than this, Doran also wrote that, "it should also be understood that the suggested acronym doesn't mean that every objective written will have all five criteria." This statement also has not followed the directives as they have entered the fray. Other curriculum experts simply say that "Objectives should be measurable,"[9] and then go on to explain why they think this is the case. These important follow-up delimiting statements by Doran are like lost scrolls, they are seldom seen connected with the circulated curriculum scriptures.

Saying that good educators should always try to measure good objectives is a very different thing than saying that a good objective is always measurable. The former leans into good reason and tells us to try to make sure we keep tabs on our level of success, while the latter tells us to only choose certain objectives to begin with – those that can be measured (which is basically none of the "acceptance" side of learning).

This probably makes sense, given the business orientation that may naturally fit with the administration of nearly anything, but it doesn't follow that it should be uncritically accepted. And, quite frankly, that is what I see happen in every case. Someone will say something like "we need to make sure these are smart objectives," and everyone else will simply shift gears and try to accommodate that sentiment.

Motivational Immediacy in Curriculum Design

Having laid out some of these hazards, there are ways to mitigate them if not eliminate them altogether. I mentioned above that real-world constraints often require less than optimal applications, and there are circumstances where large-scale curriculum design and an instructor pool are required. Military training is an example of this, due largely to its size and need to standardize. Extremely large corporations are next in line as candidates likely to need some sort of similar process. When this is necessary, the negative effects can still be mitigated, but the first stop for the leader is determine whether or not there really is a need to handle the workplace training division this way. Most often, much smaller companies are simply dressing for the job they want, or following the lead of the "big guys" and handling their training in inefficient and ineffective ways. Following are some practical considerations and steps to take to first try to eliminate the hazards and, if not possible, mitigate them effectively to promote more motivational immediacy and, because of this, more authentic learning.

Eliminate or Mitigate the Hazards

1. *Consider the Option of Changing the Way you Manage Curriculum Decisions*

The first step is to check the assumptions you may have about how your training needs to be run. The vast majority of business are on the smaller size and do not include thousands of employees spanning the country or world. If you are able to localize your training and have the instructional expert also design the curriculum for the employee learners, have the courage to step out and do it. There is nothing wrong with having a professional-looking curriculum, but the best curriculum is always going to be the one that focuses on learners and learning first, rather than form and aesthetics and rules.

A curriculum drafted on a cocktail napkin will be more effective than a formally drafted, rule-following, template-adhering curriculum design, so long as it has at its heart the notion that in the hands of the skilled facilitator, leader, and instructor, it will connect with the heart and soul of the individual learner (all of them), and lead them to a consensus for whatever shared vision stands at the center of it. Here again, is a need for training to be seen as leadership – getting someone to learn something in a classroom is always, in the end, about drawing others to you in a collaboration over a shared vision for the future. Whether that vision is grand in scale (i.e., become a fortune 500 company), or simply a mundane step along the way (complete Form 236a properly), the only effective way to succeed is to bring the learner to see the value of your vision and to join in of their own volition because they think it is a good idea.

2. *Consider Hiring Different Types of Professionals or Develop the Existing Ones*

   This might require hiring better-equipped instructors, or, in the event that is not workable, to provide the necessary education for the instructor so that they might better understand human learning.

3. *Write it Like a Leader*

   I have said all along that there is power in joining the ideas of leadership to the practices of educating and training. Redraft all curriculum (tall order) from the ground up, as though the task was one of leadership instead of transmitting sterile content (it never is sterile, actually). If you are someone who is deeply interested in becoming a powerful leader, first, you probably already are, and second, you have read lots of books and/or listened to lots of podcasts on the qualities of good leadership and effective leaders. You will have noticed that every one of these is saturated with motivational language, appeals to abiding personal connections with individuals, and words like "charisma," "magnetism," and "connection." And, of course, we "eat this stuff up" because it resonates deep inside.

   The standard training texts, however, sing a very different tune. In most cases they are shot through with clinical, technical, and impersonal information on how best to convey material in a way that will be retained (a word we have come to use as a stand-in for buy into and envision, which are more like leadership words). To know how to do what I am suggesting here, simply take the primary learning objectives that are already existing in the curriculum, take them out, think about them from the perspective of leading people in those directions, and write them again as a leader would. Yes, this is heresy, but it also is effective, especially if you want effectual learning in the short- and long-term.

4. *Leave Space for the Learner*
Curriculum is about the someone (that is becoming tiresome, right?). This phrase will keep appearing in these discussions because if the entire thing had to be only one sentence long, that would be the sentence. Everything else is just a break-down and elucidation of that one simple thought. When drafting curriculum, think of a person you are trying to persuade about something you care deeply about, with each line you draft. If the document you are drafting would not work with your significant other or informally with your co-worker on the 9th hole, then scrap it. It won't work with anyone in the classroom either because they are someone's significant other, or co-worker at some metaphorical 9th hole with someone.
   Here is a startling truth – the reason we have so much trouble getting training to work in real life is because we treat it as though it is not real life. So, perhaps the best thing to say here is to leave space for the learner as you build a curriculum and act like the task you are set upon is taking place in real life. That will solve a great many of the hazards mentioned above. Remember, I said this would be heresy.

5. *Allow (and expect) a Shadow Curriculum*
When the instructor is using the curriculum to teach a roomful of individuals, one should not only permit them but also expect them to be "boots on the ground" and to bend, twist, and rearrange the curriculum so that its essence (the content is important, for sure), is best facilitated, absorbed, and accepted with passion by the individual learners in that room. This does not mean, of course, that an individual instructor should be able to change the content itself, or to abandon the essence of the objectives, but if you hire the right instructors and develop them well, this won't be a problem. A well-educated instructor sees it as a professional challenge and passion to accurately achieve buy-in and a shared vision with each and every learner in each and every classroom. Only those who have not been equipped to know and do better, or perhaps a few subversive people, actively part from the essence of a training objective, because to do so means that they are not very good at their job. And, the small group of potentially subversive individuals are probably already doing this without permission anyway.

This is why it is so important to understand the concepts of motivational immediacy, think and act like a leader, and build all of this from the ground up. Get your ducks in a row and they will swim in a straight line.

Who Is Driving the Bus

A simple mental check of each aspect of your training and development division curriculum can provide an easy recognition of something that needs to be changed – who is driving the bus here? If the rules of curriculum design are driving the bus, get off it. If the content is driving the bus, get off it. If the legal department (ouch) is driving the bus, get off it. Some professional rules of design might be good, accurate content is always important, and legal counsel is there for a reason. They should all be on the bus and, to be fair, if they are missing, you need to go back and get them. However, if anything other than the fostering of a shared vision with the individual learner is driving the bus, fire the driver and get a new one – the new driver might not be dressed quite as nicely, or be as pleasant to look at, but you will have a safer ride and, most importantly, you will actually get to the destination you set out for.

Notes

1 Illeris, K. (2017). *How we learn: Learning and non-learning in school and beyond* (2nd ed.). Routledge.
2 Pulliam, J. D., & Van Patten, J. J. (2003). *History of education in America* (p. 71). Merrill Prentice Hall.
3 Maritain, J. (1943). *Education at the crossroads* (pp. 3, 14). Yale University Press.
4 Waugh, C. K., & Gronlund, N. E. (2013). *Assessment of student achievement* (10th ed.). Pearson.
5 Dick, W., Carey, L., & Carey, J. (2009). *The systematic design of instruction* (7th ed.). Merrill/Pearson. https://doi.org/10.1007/s11031-006-9028-7
6 Caffarella, R. S. (2002). *Planning programs for adult learners: A practical guide for educators, trainers, and staff developers* (2nd ed., p. 159). Jossey-Bass.
7 Drucker, P. F. (1954). *The practice of management.* Harper & Row.
8 Doran, G. T. (1981). There's a S.M.A.R.T. way to write management's goals and objectives. *Management Review*, *70*, 35–36.
9 Beebe, S. A., Mottet, T. P., & Roach, K. D. (2013). *Training and development: Communicating for success* (2nd ed., p. 85). Pearson.

Section III

Navigating Complications

Motivational Immediacy in the Real World

Chapter 10

F2F, Distance, and Motivational Immediacy

The Stark Truth

The advent of online and distance learning has taken a turn and is so far up the entrance ramp and onto the highway that it is not worth any real consideration of whether it is a good thing or a bad thing. There is plenty of this sort of conversation, but it can't be taken very seriously for anyone who has both feet in the everyday working world. A useful conversation, however, can center around its pros and cons, around when it should be used and how, and importantly, when it should be avoided. The purview of this topic here is how face-to-face, in-person learning, and all forms of distance learning should be viewed through the lens of motivational immediacy, street-smart motivation, and effectual learning.

There is no point in thinking through this area of practice if one is not going to be clear and honest and let the cards fall where they may. I will begin here with a series of 10 questions for you, the reader, to think over and answer honestly. You don't need to answer out loud or publicly (heads down and eyes closed…), but if you are serious about being an expert and leader in the workplace and training areas, you really do need to answer them. At the end of this chapter, I will provide my own observations. By the time we get there, however, some of what I am going to share will already be obvious to you based on how you answer the following questions.

A Few Questions

1. When you have joined zoom meetings with several people in the zoom room, did you pay more or less attention than you would have in a physical room with the boss looking at you across the room or down the table. Did you feel more free to do other stuff? Did you turn the camera off? Were you allowed to do this or not? If you were not allowed, why?
2. What have your colleagues, friends, family (kids too) said about how they behave in these online environments?

DOI: 10.4324/9781003482079-13

3. When you had to take some form of asynchronous (non-zoom) course online, did you find that you were digging-in to the deeper meaning of what was being shared, or mainly focusing on the main thoughts so you could pass the quiz. Do you ever walk away during the video and come back just to take the quiz? Do you ever think that you can just take the quiz multiple times until you get it right? Over time, has your online course developer begun to find tricky ways to make it so you have to pay attention (i.e., pausing the video for questions along the way, etc.)? Why do you think someone is getting paid to take the time to do this?
4. If you really had to persuade a friend or family member to get on board with an idea you had, would you want to talk to them in person, or shoot them an email or text? Why did you make the choice that you did? Did you have a strong preference with your answer?
5. How good was the social interaction when you last took an online course of some sort in the workplace? Was it the same as previous in-person classes you have had?
6. Do you feel that people are apt to walk away from an online course with the view that the instructor was the best that they have ever had and someone they see as a mentor?
7. Are any of these answers different when asked about in-person classes you have had in the past? Should they be? Could they be?
8. If you were the new CEO of a company and wanted to revive everyone's spirits, re-engage them in the passion for a unified vision for the future, and facilitate team-building skills, would you opt for using an in-person setting, a zoom session, or a digital recording of some sort – IF you were able to logistically do any of the three in a reasonable way? Why?
9. If you were in charge of relaying somewhat rote or technical content to a group of employees, and you knew that they largely needed the material and were interested, would you choose to share it digitally or in traditional in-person sessions? Why?
10. Do you see any patterns to your answers above? What do those patterns tell you? What are the implications of those patterns? What can you do about it in your area of control at work now or in the future? Will you do it? Why or why not?

A Few Observations

Hopefully, after getting about halfway through the above questions, you realized that it was not my intention to lead you strongly in one direction or the other. I am, perhaps, running a real risk that you will answer your own questions and then not read any further, but that is okay. It is okay because if one has really grasped the nature of human learning motivation shared so far, and if one answers these questions honestly and draws reasonable conclusions from them, you will have sorted the whole thing out as well as I could sort it out for you. The real question for the debate is how do we best leverage the different instructional modalities we have for the ends we desire. In other words, how to we make sure our means are as closely aligned with our desired end as possible? This would be means-end-fusion, it would be motivational immediacy in practice. The thoughtful, well-reasoned, intentional, and starkly honest response to this question in the workplace will go a very long way to increasing the power of our training programs and leadership efforts. Here is one final question to ask yourself:

Think of the online training that your organization uses and identify what percentage (out of 100%) each factor influences the choice to have that training online.

- It is more cost-effective, at least in the long-run.
- It is a better use of the time that we get from our employees (including instructors).
- It is generally more convenient for some or all of those involved.
- It will actually foster a much more authentic, long-term, adoption of a shared vision for our workplace (better learning)?

It is true that I think I know what the preponderance of everyone will answer here, if answering honestly, but the fact is, it doesn't really matter because I can't know that I am right about any given training effort. Research has shown remarkably mixed results about online training and this is because human learning is messy and not one sort of learning need is ever the same. Likewise, no group every gathered together in any form has ever been the same. Even the same group gathered together on two different occasions is not the same. There are no easy answers, but there is careful analysis, clearly set end-goals, and purposefully chosen means that will most effectively meet those ends, and in the shortest time possible. Being motivationally immediate is more about the process you use to make the decision than it is about the decision you make.

In truth, *one of the most significant contributions that online and distance education has made to the teaching and learning world is demonstrating just how differently we should be teaching our in-person courses.* There was inevitable push-back in our universities and in the workplace when courses started being pushed online (usually against the will of the faculty and instructors). This gradually gave way to a quieter form of acquiescence over time, likely for a number of different reasons. For one thing, it became obvious early on that the boats had been mostly burned and there was no plan to go back to where everyone was before. For another, those teaching online began, perhaps reluctantly, to see some of the conveniences of being able to work on a much more flexible timeline and have greater freedom from being hemmed up for a given set of times each week for an extended season.

For those in upper management and those paying the bills, there was undoubtedly a financial benefit, at least in the long-run, so time was given space to run its course. The question that slowly but surely became obvious over time, as instructors and learners alike started to make their own decisions about being a part of an online course or an in-person course, was this – what are we doing in the classroom that makes it worth getting dressed, put together, driving to the location, and sitting there in a fixed position for hours? Why would anyone sit in a room and listen to someone drone on about something when they could do the same exact thing but with (a) volume control, (b) fast-forward, (c) rewind, and (d) mute, at their fingertips? Said this way, might there be some inherent weaknesses with distance learning options? Can they be mitigated?

This was a tipping point for many. It just wasn't worth the effort for the larger percentage of learners to do more work to get the same exact thing. For many of those teaching, this was a wake-up call to get busy fostering learning together in person in ways that simply couldn't be replicated online; to make learners feel like they were missing out on something better if they stayed at home. If done well, really dynamic in-person learning experiences were often worth the inconvenience of going there in person, while mediocre, lecture-based sermonizing never was to begin with. I have a colleague who is fond of saying "a bad lecture is always a bad lecture." It is likewise true that a bad in-person class is always a bad class. One ought not to confuse the quality with the modality.

The take-aways here are simple but can be game-changing. There are seven main suggestions I will address here but there are more that could be produced with some dialogue with those around you.

1. **Adapt your teaching to the form you are teaching it in.**
   If you make everyone come together in a physical location, don't take up most of the time showing cool videos that they could watch online in their living room, barefoot, with a fun drink. If you are in-person, work the room, facilitate lots of interpersonal contact, group discussions, and collaborative thinking. This is a space where you can really see the fruit of your own natural (and learned) charisma and leadership skill. Teach like a leader. Do not do the same thing online and in-person, or one of those two formats is the wrong one for what you are doing. The content may be similar, but how you go about it should certainly be different.

2. **Know the limitations of each.**
No, they are not equally good for all things. And, no, the content isn't going to be exactly the same when you deliver it in very different ways. Remember, human learning is not simply the clinical transfer of content. In fact, it is never merely the transfer of clinical content. It is the sharing of a vision with others in the hope that they will understand that vision, appreciate it, learn as much as they can about it, and then join the effort to bring it about in the workplace. Be aware of the limitations and inherent weaknesses and make a plan to design them out, or, if not possible, to weaken their potential to damage the learning situation.
3. **Where possible choose the right modality for the right sort of thing.**
All learning is not the same, therefore all training is not the same. Both the nature of the content and the nature of the learner are moving targets that come together in any given learning environment creating a phenomenon that is a great deal less predictable that we would like to believe. If you are trying to convey routine technical knowledge (content) to a group of learners who you are very sure are generally interested (are very aware that they need it to do their job), distance modalities may work very effectively and efficiently.
At the university, for instance, after years of faculty claiming that of all things, statistics should not be taught online, I have begun to hear more than one student share that the online courses (with good faculty, that is) were much easier for statistics because they could watch the short videos over and over, pause, skip, etc. These are things that they could never do in an in-person class meeting. In this sense, no one is left behind trying to catch up during a lecture. Couple this with an instructor who is willing to be available outside of the course for clarification and help, and you have a superior learning situation where it was once thought impossible.
Before going on here, take a minute and consider how different this mention of the "rewind, pause, and fast-forward" options are for learning than the one up above. The one above seemed so clearly like a reason to avoid online teaching at all, while this one makes it sound like something every good learner needs and can use to their advantage. Both are true. That is why the hard work for the educator and leader is to take all factors into considerations, avoid set, across-the-board decisions, and keep the end out in front of every means at all times.
Conversely, if you are teaching something that really requires something akin to a religious conversion on the part of the employee, a series of short videos with some "take as many times as you need" quizzes will likely come up short, especially since at least half of them will have their

phone at the grill with them, watching it (sort of) while they are grilling steaks and having a beer.

4. **Match the right sort of person up to teach the right sort of class for them.**
   It took me a while to come to terms with this one. After many years of teaching both online and in person, I have to be honest with myself and say that it is not a good fit with my own personality, skills, and passion, to teach online. That doesn't mean that I can't or shouldn't do it from time to time. In fact what it really means, is that there are others who might be really good at the things that I am not good at, and therefore, I can't use my own weaknesses to judge the whole online modality itself.

   I have said in another book that online formats can sometimes provide an even greater chance to communicate one on one with individual students (something very good for motivational immediacy), but to be honest, the amount of time it takes to do that (think about having 25 pen pals all writing complex, very detailed and technical emails to you every week), makes it difficult to do it right. I like the energy and dynamics of being with people in a room, seeing their faces, and reading their moment-by-moment expressions. Sometimes our working environments have all of us doing the thing we enjoy the least and are the worst at. There is power in cross-training for sure, and we all need to be team players, which means taking one for the team from time to time. However, as a general practice for motivational immediacy and street-smart motivation, allocating the right resources to the right task is good practice.
5. **Consider your Primary Objective.**
   One thing that is brilliantly clear in light of the idea of motivational immediacy in teaching, learning, and leading, is that means should be best suited for their ends. That requires us to be honest about the ends on the first place. Is the desired end authentic, long-term, employee buy-in? Is the desired end simply a legal record of having told everyone they should or should not do a certain thing? Don't answer that last one out loud, please. Is the desired end simply and only about money? It is true that a good leader must take legal efficacies into account and that financial means are scarce and must be used wisely, but the question to ask yourself is how much of each of those factors weighing in on the decision that is being made. If it is about learning, make sure that one is the heavy-hitter in every decision you make and only cave to the other two when (a) there is no other choice, or (b) they happen to coincide with the educational power of the choice to begin with. One can remember Steven Covey's admonition to "keep the main thing the main thing."[1]

6. **Never, absolutely never do anything at all because it is what everyone else is doing.**
   There is nothing more to say about this one, except that it is not a joke.
7. **If there are other reasons (i.e., legal) you are going to use an online format, own it, don't provide disingenuous answers to yourself or those you lead.**
   These types of decisions are never easy and are always fraught with risk. It is not always expedient to share all of the inner workings of your decisions with everyone else in the workplace, but if you want to be the strongest leader that you are able to be, you absolutely must never be dishonest with *yourself*. And, as you may remember someone telling you when you were a child – lying by omission counts as a lie. It probably never occurred to any of us that as adults *that* particular type of dishonesty would be the weapon of choice used by our egos. Motivational immediacy can come through and shine brightly in nearly any type of teaching format, but it can only every show through one type of process and that is one that is intentional, well-reasoned, and made in an effort to reach for a clearly stated desired end.

Note

1 Covey, S. (2020). The seven habits of highly effective people. Simon & Schuster.

Chapter 11

Measuring Effectual Learning in the Workplace

For many, it is easy to get excited about some of these ideas, and it should be – they are empirically based and effective. However, this excitement can be short lived when one returns to work and is asked to provide some sort of measurable evidence that any specific methods are beneficial and worth the investment. Chapter 9 shares some information on the contemporary emphasis placed on measurement, and it weighs heavily on all areas of the teaching and learning continuum in the workplace.

Training departments are being asked to operate as "profit centers" and being asked to "provide documentation of the value added as a result of their services."[1] Despite the discussion in Chapter 9 about the severely negative effects of allowing measurement constraints to drive training practices, there remains a clear need to, as best we are able, measure the relative effectiveness of our training programs, and of employee knowledge and skills in the workplace. The question is not whether measurement is important, or whether it should be attempted, but to what extent it can be done well and to what extent it is limited in precision and accuracy. Using some of the language we have been using throughout, one could say that measurement should not be the primary objective, effectual learning should. Secondary objectives can be very important, but they cannot be permitted to trip up the primary. Maintaining the order of priorities of such objectives is motivationally immediate.

Short-Term vs. Long-Term Measurement

Despite the importance of measurement, it cannot be allowed to dictate bad practice. For instance, because the ability to measure learning has become so important, teaching content has been oriented almost entirely around behavioral outcomes. This, at first glance, may not be problematic, but in practice, it has been exactly that. The sorts of behavioral outcomes that we want are the consistent, accurate, and reliable application

DOI: 10.4324/9781003482079-14

of learned material in the everyday lived experience of the working world. This is referred to, among other things, as learning transfer. However, those sorts of behavioral outcomes are long-term objectives and, while measurable, come long after the training has taken place. In the training classroom, any sort of behavioral objective is typically and of necessity measured in an entirely unauthentic manner and is at best a waste of time, and at worst, damaging to every aspect of life that touches it.

A long-term behavior objective might be something like – "employee wears hardhat while present in the manufacturing area of the warehouse." This is fair enough. However, measuring this takes lots of time and, by necessity, comes after the training, not during it. In this sense, I would say that this sort of long-term measurement is entirely compatible with the concepts of motivational immediacy and effectual learning.

What is most often trickled down into instructional practice, however, is something very different from this. What has become the norm in practice is the short-term behavioral objective. The difference is profound. Here is the difference: a long-term behavioral objective is an employee actually wearing their hardhat in the workspace, while a short-term behavioral objective is the same employee indicating their knowledge of the rule by indicating a "B" on the in-class or online assessment.

What is interesting, and perhaps sad, about this, is that while both are indeed behavioral objectives that are related to the behavior of wearing a hardhat in the workspace, the long-term behavioral objective is measuring the behavior of wearing the hat, while the short-term objective is measuring the employee's behavior to circle the "B" on the quiz. Said this way, the whole thing seems sort of foolish, and, at risk of sounding flippant, it is. They are not the same thing.

If we are not able to measure the employee wearing the hat for real (think real-world training here), then we must measure the employee's heartfelt (not brain-acknowledged) intention to wear the helmet in the future. That is, either we only measure the future behavior in the future, or we measure the learner's heartfelt commitment to engage in the future behavior as of now.

The stark truth of this entire premise can be easily seen in the anecdote of a Sunday school teacher in a Protestant church operating on formal curricular learning objectives: "given a list of the 10 commandments, the student will correctly identify the 7th one." In this scenario, the teacher has created a measurable, behavioral objective, but what that teacher really wants is for her charges to know that stealing is morally wrong. The measurable objective in this case falls a great deal short of the true long-term behavior objective.

None of this, however, reduces the importance in our contemporary societal context, of being able to measure the positive effects of anything we are proposing that might require either significant change, significant cost, or some combination of the two. There needs to be some way forward.

Limited Ability to Measure Effectual Learning

It is important to know that a training program is working, and although current behaviorally based assessments are quite good at indicating a particular kind of effectiveness, they do little to inform how well training programs are resulting in *effectual learning*. Engaging in motivational immediacy at all of the related levels that are required to do it well from the curriculum design process all the way through to the jobsite, is difficult, time-consuming work. Since time is often money, it can be seen as a financial burden.

The theory, concepts, and empirical work represented in the preceding chapters come together to make a strong case that in the long-run, training programs that result in effectual learning will always be less costly than those that do not. This is because cheaper programs that do not result in training transfer cost the company both wasted money and prolonged inefficiency in production and services.

When digging into this topic, there is a fundamental truth about measurement that should be noted – *not being able to measure something perfectly is not the same thing as not being able to measure something at all.*

The Job Dictates the Grain Size

What we use to measure something depends not only on what the thing is, but on what our purpose is in measuring it in the first place. In other areas of life, this makes a great deal of sense without a great deal of discussion. When someone is trying to set up a training room with standard eight-foot tables, it may be completely sufficient to pace of the length of the room, rounding one's shoe size up or down to one foot. This is particularly true if there will be a significant margin of space in the front and back, or sides of the room.

Conversely, it would be difficult to find someone who thinks simply pacing off a distance is sufficient for the purpose pouring the footers for a house. *The purpose of the measurement dictates how precise it must be.* So too, does the purpose of training efforts dictate just how precise a measurement has to be in order to serve its purpose and provide the necessary answer. When a measurement that may be the equivalent of "pacing off a distance" is sufficient to answer the question at hand, but extensive conversations, arguments, and instructional method-shifts occur, this is an indication that measurement has become about measurement, just like curriculum has become about curriculum, and training has become about content.

If the overarching purpose of the entire training enterprise is to foster some sort of employee learning for the extended purpose of long-term training transfer, then training, curriculum, and measurement are all, in the end, about *people*. This particular line of argument about how precise measurement needs to be is extremely important because in the case of adopting motivational immediacy practices, ***the measurement only needs to be precise enough to show improvement beyond that of practices as they are.*** This will not be difficult so long as – and this is key – the training professional remains focused on what, exactly, the other measures were measuring to begin with. After all, a good measure that measures an unimportant thing is not nearly as valuable as a poor measure that provides an index for something vital.

Effectual learning is not merely about making sure that someone knows how to do something, but about facilitating a situation where they feel as though they *should* do it. And, going even beyond this, to a place where they will do it. There is a legitimate reason why someone might want to measure, to the best of their ability, whether the new methods being implemented are worth the effort of implementing them. The following information is simply one suggestion for doing so.

Theory of Planned Behavior (TPB) and the Measurement of Effectual Learning

In the late 1970s, Fishbein and Ajzen introduced his Theory of Reasoned Behavior,[2,3] which Azjen later developed into the TPB.[4,5] The TPB has been shown to have predictive value for human behavior over and beyond a mere indication from an individual of intent. TPB uses inventory scales to measure variables such as the intentions, perceived behavioral control, subjective norms, and normative beliefs of an individual. These variables, taken together, provide a powerful tool to predict future behavior.

This contribution filled a gap because someone's verbal indication that they will take a certain action in the future is not effectively predictive of whether they will actually do it. By adding these additional factors, the application of Ajzen's theory was able to achieve a greatly increased predictability for the future action.

The TPB has been used in a number of different practical ways to predict specific ranges of behavior. For example, it has been used in a predictive way in relation to sleep-deprived driving,[6,7] walking behavior,[8] Anorexia Nervosa,[9] entrepreneurial intentions,[10,11] nursing care,[12] and recycling behaviors.[13] It has also been examined to test the predictive power in the context of communication. Researchers conducted a study with communication professionals and used TPB to predict measurement and evaluation efforts and in light of the results specifically emphasized the potential relevance to educational efforts.[14]

One drawback of using the TPB in educational settings is that there would frequently be a strong incentive to be deceptive when completing it. In the case of the truck drivers, there would be very good reasons for a driver to avoid indicating that he was not going to be obeying the law or following required regulations. This sort of response bias would render the results invalid, defeating the purpose. However, when the person completing the inventory is permitted to do so anonymously, without any identifiers, physical or digital, being collected and connected, much of this bias could be avoided.

Administering the TPB inventory anonymously would make it impracticable to use it to assess the learner in any constructive way, but it could be very valuable in assessing the teaching and learning situation itself. Finding out after a course is finished that 8 out of 10 participants did *not* buy-in to the content and will *not* be using it at any point in the future would be immensely important for the educator.

If the TPB provides a way to measure the level of learner acceptance of content, and the acquisition of the content may be measured in the conventional ways, it would be possible to measure what I have been referring to as effectual learning (acquisition of content + acceptance of content). Taking some standardized form of these two measurements and combining could provide a concrete, quantifiable coefficient or index for effectual learning. It would not be a precise measurement, but it would be precise enough to tell the informed leader with resource concerns that it is worth the outlay.

Learning Efficiency Index

Although it would be very useful to have some form of objective read on effectual learning, being able to measure the *relative* efficiency of a given learning situation would be more powerful. In order to do this, one would need to have an index of effectual learning (benefit) that can be divided into an index of the overall outlay of the educational effort (cost). This sort of formula would allow for a scalable index that could be used for educational initiatives ranging from very small, one-time episodes, to large-scale, multiple-year initiatives.

The Formula

The formula shown in Figure 11.1 shows an example of the learning efficiency index. The numerator contains two numbers, the *acceptance coefficient* and the *acquisition coefficient*. Each is assigned a range of 1–5, with

5 being the highest level in the range. The numerator is divided by the denominator to derive a relative efficiency coefficient.

The denominator of the formula indicates two types of educational outlays – *direct financial costs* and *person-hour costs.* In most if not all cases, there is also a direct financial cost for the person-hours and a decision has to be made whether to add the direct financial cost of the person-hours or to the direct financial side, but the person-hour cost in this formula represents the relative magnitude of hours required for the educational initiative and, in a sense, the labor opportunity cost, rather than fiscal cost, of those hours. The ranges here are the same as for the numerator above but are reversed, ranging from 5 to 1, indicating the highest to lowest cost in the respective areas.

The combined score of the numerator (effectual learning) could range from 2 to 10, and the denominator (combined cost) from 10 to 2. The combined *learning efficiency ratio* score then could range from 0.2 to 5.0, with the higher number indicating a greater degree of efficiency.

Figure 11.2 contains three examples of effectual learning and efficiency calculations to lend clarity. I will expand on a few of them here. In the first example, the denominator consists of a 4 for person-hour costs, and a 3 for financial costs, for a total of 7. Taking the numerator (effectual learning) from above (6) and putting it over the denominator from the same example (7) the ratio would be 6/7 or .857, indicating a relatively low efficiency, since the scale ranges from .2 to 5.0, with 5 being the most efficient.

In the second example in Figure 11.2, you have the highest level of effectual learning (10) over the lowest level of work hour and financial cost (2), which results in a Learning Efficiency Index of "5" which is the highest potential score. Example three shows the exact opposite, with the lowest possible effectual learning score (2) over the highest possible cost score (10), which results in a learning efficiency index of ".2" which is the lowest possible score.

Keep in mind that the level from 1 to 5 indicated for the work-intensive score is a relative score, not a raw score, and can be easily applied to an extremely wide range of training programs. For instance, if one engages in semester-long employee development courses and the number of dedicated hours is in the hundreds, the range of 1–5 can be applied to it as well as to a one-time 45-minute in-service course that requires 3–4 hours of preparation. In both cases, a choice of 1 would indicate a low level of work *relative to that particular project size*, and as such is a quasi-standardized score. Purely abstract examples are limited so in the final section of this chapter, a more concrete example will be provided, one with a high learning efficiency coefficient and the other with a low one.

$$\frac{Acquisition\,(1-5) + Acceptance\,(1-5)}{Work\ Hours\,(5-1) + Fiscal\ Costs\,(5-1)} = Learning\ Efficiency\ Index$$

Figure 11.1 Effectual Learning and Learning Efficiency Index Formula.
Note: *Range of .2–5 (Higher indicates a higher degree of learning efficiency).

$$\frac{Acquisition\,(5) + Acceptance\,(1)}{Work\ Hours\,(4) + Fiscal\ Costs\,(3)} = \frac{6}{7} = .857$$

$$\frac{Acquisition\,(5) + Acceptance\,(5)}{Work\ Hours\,(1) + Fiscal\ Costs\,(1)} = \frac{10}{2} = 5.0$$

$$\frac{Acquisition\,(1) + Acceptance\,(1)}{Work\ Hours\,(5) + Fiscal\ Costs\,(5)} = \frac{2}{10} = 0.2$$

Figure 11.2 Three Examples of the Learning Efficiency Index.

The Case of the Somewhat Efficient Logistics Tracking System (LTS) Training

Consider a mandated in-service training program for the organization's LTS. The organization had recently switched to LTS and the scheduled training was part of the transitional process to migrate to the new system. Employees were sent an email telling them that they were required to complete online LTS training by a certain date. The informational email also laid out some basic information. The online training consisted of about 15 different modules that ranged in length from 5 to 12 minutes. Employees could complete this training from any location so long as they had internet access. The training was entirely automated but also interactive. It consisted of brilliantly produced videos and required technical exercises which required the employees to work in the LTS and demonstrate certain selective functions that were being taught in the lesson.

Behind the Scenes

There were employees who closely watched the videos, completed all of the exercises, and went beyond that, spending time outside of the training messing around with the stuff they had learned. But time was tight. So, most employees simply put the thing on autopilot and did other things, while the videos were playing. The IT personnel involved in producing the training were on to this trick and had worked to mitigate it ahead of time. They had built in a pause every few minutes so if a participant walked away for more than a few minutes it would wait for them to return. Going even further than this, occasional questions were asked in little pop-up boxes and missing too much just prior to it could be a problem. All of this required that employees not wander too far or "check out" too much.

Using the Formula

The learning efficiency formula was computed for the training as a whole (see Figure 11.3). The administrators and personnel from the training department that made it a requirement and developed it, assigned a Work Hour Cost of 4 (out of 5) because the production hours required for the videos, tests, and other technical aspects was very high. The Fiscal costs were set at 3 because although the cost was high, it was cheaper than it would have been to pay all of the employees to be out of service for an entire day in a single location. That provided a total cost of 7.

Taking the data from the tests that were embedded in the online training, a high score of 5 was assigned to the acquisition side of things. This was due in part to the fact that employees had to answer all questions correctly in order to move forward. But when an anonymous survey was administered to all employees across the organization, using the TPB and measuring whether or not employees were intending to utilize all of the content that was transmitted to them, it was found that the majority of employees indicated that they had no intention of using the great majority of the features that were covered because first, they did not have the time to do so, and secondly (a related issue), they reported that they had learned all of the content in a way that was entirely unconnected to their own questions, interests, needs, and work production habits and would not be able to remember how to do any of it. Many also were honest enough to indicate that they didn't actually watch most of it. These results led the administrators to assign an acceptance value of 1.

Plugging in the numbers to the formula ended up with the following numbers: 6/7 = .86 learning efficiency index coefficient (range of 0.2–5.0). This is not an impressive value.

$$\frac{Acquisition\,(5) + Acceptance\,(1)}{Work\ Hours\,(4) + Fiscal\ Costs\,(3)} = \frac{6}{7} = .86$$

Figure 11.3 Efficiency Index Formula Example # 1.

Note: *Range of .2–5 (Higher indicates a higher degree of learning efficiency).

The Case of the More Efficient LTS Training

Consider the same basic training program for the organization's LTS. Rather than being online, the training is scheduled for a full 8-hour day with lunch provided. The decision was made to offer lunch, adding to the fiscal costs, because of the location of the training facility and the limited time for a lunch break based on the amount of content deemed necessary to cover.

The training consisted of having nearly 75 employees gather in a large room and, using laptops, follows the instructions of the facilitator in the front. There was much grumbling about the required day of training, and when the employees arrived to the training it was fair to assume that they were not excited, as a whole, nor were they engaged with the experience.

The facilitator at the front surprised everyone by having them get into groups of 3–5 and to discuss the following:

- What types of things do you like to do in the LTS?
- What types of things do you often have trouble with?
- What types of things would you do if you could do them easily?
- What are some questions you have always had but never gone to the trouble of asking about?

After about 20 minutes of talking in groups (each group was told to select a "scribe" and spokesperson to report out), the facilitator called everyone back to order and asked for one of the groups to shout out one of the questions. Someone from a group on the left side of the room spoke up and said, "one of the questions that came up in our group is about why we need to go to the trouble of selecting 'no' or 'n/a' for all of the fields where there is not something specific to enter. It takes time and is a complete waste. Why can't it be set up so that we only need to add something if there is something to add? Why not just set 'no' or 'n/a' as a default?"

The facilitator said, "great! Let's talk about that. First, how many of you had a question that was related to that one?" about seven other hands went up around the room. "Okay," she said, "let's talk about this for a bit." Then, she led the entire group in a discussion about the pros and cons of such a move and why it may have been set up the way it is. Somewhere along the line, someone pointed out that if there was a default of "no" or "n/a" and someone forgot to make an entry, it would be impossible to know because "no" is an answer itself (albeit the wrong one in that case). If it is left blank, then at least it is obvious that someone didn't complete the fields.

Someone else pointed out that although that made sense, it also didn't because if everyone just got frustrated and left them blank anyway, it became an assumption that the answer was "no." Otherwise, it was pointed out, a "yes" would have been entered. In the commonly accepted practice, no news was, essentially, good news.

This discussion had several effects. First, it provided very good information to the instructor, which could be used to improve both the system and the cultural practices surrounding it. Second, it allowed the employees to think through the effects of their decisions on others, to see the other side of things, and to hear at least some of their fellow-workers provide reasons to do it the way it is *supposed* to be done. The net effect of all of this was a general attitude shift toward having to check the box, and a feeling of having been able to give their opinions and be heard. Not everyone agreed with the decision, but most everyone now understood it and also realized that everyone couldn't be happy with either choice, even though one had to be made.

After this, the facilitator continued to work around the room and answer questions. *However, she did have a master list of learning objectives and referred to it constantly so that she could connect every one of the objectives to the questions that were being asked.* For the few objectives that remained at the end (the ones she couldn't figure out how to connect with participant questions), she addressed by having everyone get together in groups again and work on discussing some carefully constructed questions that would develop at least a temporary need-to-know among participants.

Behind the Scenes

Many of the employees went into the situation with the normal skeptical attitude toward a full day of training. Attitudes were not optimal overall, and expectations were low. This is not because the employees at this organization are particularly grumpy or cynical people, just that they are responsible for quite a lot of work and generally struggle, like many of us, just to keep up and survive.

But as the day wore on, attitudes improved because the facilitator was answering their specific, personally relevant questions. Even though many of them would not have gone if it were not required, there was also an attitude of making the best of it and trying to find the answers to some of the questions (or gripes) they had had for years. At the very end, the participants were required to demonstrate the ability to navigate the LTS and to use its basic functions. Groups were put into teams and had a competition for accurate procedurally correct LTS entry completions. The process was, of course, largely subjective, but all participants in the end, voted for one of the two teams because of a particularly dynamic and interesting feature they had employed within the LTS, and the process overall, was festive in nature.

Using the Formula

The learning efficiency formula was computed for the training as a whole (see Figure 11.4). The administrators and personnel from the organization that required the training and developed it assigned a Work Hour Cost of 5 (out of 5) because while the preparation time was much less, all of the employees from the entire organization had to be assembled. The Fiscal costs were set at 4 because although the technical cost was lower than the online model, it was costly to provide lunch and travel costs for some of the remote, off-site employees. That provided a total cost of 9.

Given that everyone was demonstrating their ability in the classroom immediately after being shown how to do it, a high score of 5 was assigned to the acquisition side of the house. This was due, similarly to the online model, in part to the fact that employees had peer assistance and were required to conduct the functions correctly before leaving. But when the anonymous survey was administered to all employees across the organization, using the TPB and measuring whether or not employees were intending to utilize all of the content that was transmitted to them, it was found that the majority of employees indicated that they absolutely intended on using the great majority of the features that were covered because they knew how to do things that were specifically relevant to them and how they used the system, and because they were able to interact with others in real-time, about those personally relevant questions (and answers). Simply put, they understood more clearly why the system was set up the way it was, but in relation to their own work (not in the context of some historical lesson for the sake of passing on inert knowledge). These results led the administrators to assign an acceptance value of 5.

Figure 11.4 shows that plugging in the numbers to the formula ended up with the following numbers: 10/9 = 1.11; learning efficiency index coefficient (range of 0.2–5.0).

$$\frac{\textit{Acquisition}\,(5) + \textit{Acceptance}\,(5)}{\textit{Work Hours}\,(5) + \textit{Fiscal Costs}\,(4)} = \frac{10}{9} = 1.11$$

Figure 11.4 Efficiency Index Formula Example # 2.

Note: *Range of .2–5 (Higher indicates a higher degree of learning efficiency).

Discussion of the Two Examples

The first thing I should probably say here is that my point is not at all to try to make some sort of a case that face-to-face training is, in all cases, superior. Something worth noticing here is that, in the case of the above examples, a training program that costs more in *both* work hour and fiscal costs, could actually be *more* efficient than one costing less in both ways. The exact opposite could be true also, but that is the point, really – it is a ratio of the two that determines the learning efficiency situation.

Costs could, at times, close off options for certain types of programs, and when that is the case, there is no point complaining about how much better it would be otherwise. But it is important to understand the moving parts that go into this sort of analysis and to understand that it is the effectual learning (acquire and accept) part of the learning side (numerator) that makes a great deal of difference in the efficiency coefficient. And, given that the point of the entire enterprise is some form of learning, and, by extension, training transfer, that ought to be sufficient.

The question that needs to be carefully considered is this: "is a \$5,000 course that produces very little employee change more or less cost-efficient, than a \$7,000 course that results in a significant amount of employee change?" This is not a new question, but what changes the nature of it quite a bit is shifting our conception of "employee change" away from paper tests or the performance of skills properly while being watched, and toward one where employees make internalized, long-term decisions to buy-in to those answers and skills being applied in the workplace.

Remember, the whole reason for this discussion in the first place is that administrators tend to like the idea of helping people learn better but are in need of some sort of evidence that the extra effort is worth it. Or, for more moderate but still important expectations, simply to merit a change in the way business is being done. Everyone tends to like evidence, and the training enterprise is no exception. To summarize this, the value of this formula, or perhaps a better one similar to it, is that it can establish to some extent that it is worth the effort to teach differently, because everyone learns better. It is not to justify, per se, the cheapest way to go about it.

The proposed formula here is not the final destination in this particular route of thought, but it is an example of a way forward in the face of the measurement problem. There are probably many potential pitfalls to what I have suggested but from my perspective, an inherent weakness of the formula is the *acquisition coefficient*, simply because of the inherent problem with knowledge assessment itself. In the examples above, both types of LTS training resulted in a "5.0" of acquisition simply because in both cases, success was required for each answer in order to pass/complete the course. The example was constructed this way because it seemed more "real-world" for this sort of thing. This could be a problem because simply getting a multiple-choice answer correct on a quiz doesn't mean the individual has deeply integrated that knowledge in a lasting or applicable way – even on the acquisition side. This sort of problem exists outside of the specific issue that is being addressed in this chapter and so, of course, it also exists inside it. Using assessments that require more accurate acquisition might tighten up the calculations.

This approach bears some rigorous testing for sure, but on the other hand, when nothing like it is being done at all, the measurement bar is, at least initially, low. That is, it is an area ripe for testing for any innovative and courageous instructional leaders.

Notes

1 Kraiger, K., & Jung, K. M. (1997). Linking training objectives to evaluation. In M. A. Quinones, & A. Ehrenstein (Eds.), *Training for a rapidly changing workplace: Applications of psychological research.* American Psychological Association.
2 Kraiger, K., & Jung, K. M. (1997). Linking training objectives to evaluation. In M. A. Quinones, & A. Ehrenstein (Eds.), *Training for a rapidly changing workplace: Applications of psychological research.* American Psychological Association.
3 Ajzen, I., & Fishbein, M. (1980). *Understanding attitudes and predicting social behavior.* Prentice-Hall.
4 Fishbein, M., & Ajzen, I. (1975). *Belief, attitude, intention, and behavior.* Addison-Wesley.
5 Ajzen, I. (1985). From intentions to actions: A theory of planned behavior. In J. Kuhl, & J. Beckmann (Eds.), *Action control: From cognition to behavior* (pp. 11–39). Springer-Verlag.
6 Ajzen, I. (1991). The theory of planned behavior. *Organizational Behavior and Human Decision Processes, 50*(2), 179–211.
7 Jiang, K., Ling, F., Feng, Z., Wang, K., & Shao, C. (2017). Why do drivers continue driving while fatigued? An application of the theory of planned behaviour. *Transportation Research: Part A: Policy and Practice, 98*, 141–149. https://doi.org/10.1016/j.tra.2017.02.003
8 Darker, C. D. D. (2008). *Applying the theory of planned behaviour to walking: Development and evaluation of measures and an intervention.* [Doctorates Thesis, University of Birmingham]. UB Campus Repository, UBIRA E Theses. https://etheses.bham.ac.uk/id/eprint/1433/
9 Dawson, L., Mullan, B., & Sainsbury, K. (2015). Using the theory of planned behaviour to measure motivation for recovery in anorexia nervosa. *Appetite, 84*, 309–315. https://doi.org/10.1016/j.appet.2014.10.028
10 Rueda, S., Moriano, J.A., & Liñán, F. (2015). Validating a theory of planned behavior questionnaire to measure entrepreneurial intentions. In, A. Fayolle, P. Kyro, & F. Liñán (Eds.) *Developing, shaping and growing entrepreneurship.* Edward Elger Publishing.
11 Setiaji, K. (2019). A measure of entrepreneurial behavior of university students: A theory of planned behavior approach. *Dinamika Pendidikan, 13*(2), 143–56. https://doi.org/10.15294/dp.v13i2.18327
12 Vincent, C., Riley, B. B., & Wilkie, D. J. (2015). Developing items to measure theory of planned behavior constructs for opioid administration for children: Pilot testing. *Pain Management Nursing, 16*(6), 900–909. https://doi.org/10.1016/j.pmn.2015.07.005

13 Passafaro, P., Livi, S., & Kosic, A. (2019). Local norms and the theory of planned behavior: Understanding the effects of spatial proximity on recycling intentions and self-reported behavior. *Frontiers in Psychology, 10*. https://doi.org/10.3389/fpsyg.2019

14 Buhmann, A., & Brønn, P. S. (2018). Applying Ajzen's theory of planned behavior to predict practitioners' intentions to measure and evaluate communication outcomes. *Corporate Communications: An International Journal, 23*(3), 377–391. https://doi.org/10.1108/CCIJ-11-2017-0107

Chapter 12

Ethics, and the Facilitator as Mediator

The Courage to Try New Things

This is a tricky discussion to have with the classroom instructor, the training director, and the CEO all in the room at the same time. That is because some of what will be shared here is of the type that the individuals in these different roles sometimes don't agree on. The fact is this is exactly the sort of thing that everyone should be working to find agreement on to begin with, so in many ways, if this makes sense to everyone reading it no matter what their role is in the workplace, then the case has been made.

Like all other concepts related to being motivationally immediate and fostering effectual learning, courage is required. Considering the following concept openly and engaging with the possibilities and potential opportunities, no matter what your position in the workplace will ensure that you are able to expand your capacity for leading.

The Nature of an Ethical Dilemma

This chapter is largely about how to navigate a particular type of ethical dilemma so it makes sense to talk broadly about ethical dilemmas before digging in too deeply on the matter at hand. The important thing to realize going into this is that when we talk of an ethical dilemma, we are not talking about a right vs. wrong situation. When faced with a decision between right and wrong, it may be a dilemma of some form (it might be difficult to do the right thing), but it is not what is commonly referred to as an ethical dilemma.

A proper ethical dilemma is when a person is faced with two right decisions that are or seem on the face of them, to be opposed to one another. The age-old example of this is someone asking you how you like their new outfit. In one sense, it seems like you owe them honesty and to deliver an outright, boldfaced lie while looking them in the eye seems decidedly wrong. On the another, however, it seems not quite right to tell them just

DOI: 10.4324/9781003482079-15

how awful you think the outfit is and just how bad it is making them look at the moment. This is one of those silly examples that actually demonstrates the issue precisely, if not in a very serious way. How serious this is, definitely depends on who is asking you.

An ethical dilemma could also result when one is faced with a forced decision when neither of the two options seem ethically right. Most situations could be thought of either way depending on one's outlook. It is in this tension between two morally right things that we find the context for the following concepts.

Ethical Tensions for the Training Professional

In the workplace training domain, there are likely many difficult ethical dilemmas, but there is one particular cluster that is almost always present for the training instructor. That dilemma concerns the question of which direction the instructor's loyalty should lie in. At this point, the CEO in the room has a clear answer – "the boss." And, this makes sense since it is the organization that pays the instructor to do their job. However, all good educators feel a strong ethical concern for the learners under their care and influence. That is an age-old tradition and obligation. In the long-run, no upper-level manager should ever accept any instructional staff who don't feel this strong ethical obligation to the learner – that is what makes them good at what they do, which is ultimately in the interest of the boss as well as the organization as a whole. In the face of trying to practice motivational immediacy, the strength of all of these ethical binds increases.

Three Ethical Dilemmas for the Motivationally Immediate Training Instructor

There are three primary ethical dilemmas that the motivationally immediate instructor faces in practice on a daily basis. Each of these is similar and related, but distinct. All three of these can be resolved to a large extent by applying the same strategy.

Instructor Values vs. Supervisor Values

Everyone has different values. Adding to the complexity, and also difficulty, everyone has many ways through which to implement and practice those values. Disagreements can arise over a million small things, like how training rooms should be arranged; whether PowerPoint should be used, and if so, how many slides and who gets to design them; what content, specifically, should be included, and what, if any can (or maybe even should) be skipped. Sometimes the disagreements are centered on more significant issues, like whether certain training courses should be dropped from the program; whether the instructor should have any freedom to change the ways the content is delivered, depending on the learners in the individual class session, or, perhaps the most difficult, when one of the parties, but not both, feel that a particular sort of content, or a particular teaching method is itself, unethical. These sorts of conflicts and the resultant obstructions can become a real impediment to the training professional who has determined to engage in motivational immediacy in the classroom.

Instructor Values vs. the Content

Training professionals can also regularly have difficulties specifically with the content they have been asked to teach. All of these sorts of issues are interwoven in some ways, but problems with content can manifest themselves in at least three ways.

Content vs. Interest. A common problem that is raised when talking with training professionals around the country and the world is that the training content is so uninteresting, and perhaps irrelevant, that the instructor can't stand teaching it, and therefore totally "gets" why the learner doesn't like it much either. With regard to being interested in the content, one should always "own what you teach, know why you teach it, feel deeply about its importance, and then share that honestly and directly with your students."[1] This, however, is very much easier said than done.

Content vs. Job. Nearly every training professional has at one time or another, been stuck with teaching content that seems, professionally speaking, to be at odds with the realities of the job that the employee learners actually do. That is, sometimes the training that filters down from upper levels within an organization picks up the flavoring of boardroom thinking and becomes an odd, or even, at times, dangerous fit for the employee engaged at ground level on the job.

These sorts of difficulties are serious, particularly if there are perceived concerns for safety. There is no suggestion here, of course, that such badly fitting content elements are forced upon the trainer or the employee learner with malicious or negligent intent. However, large bureaucratic systems can breed these sorts of problems, and the person often left in the awkward spot of trying to find a way to balance professional ethics, company loyalty, personal career sustainability, and a genuine care for the employee learner, is the classroom instructor.

Adding to this dynamic, the training instructor is the exact point of contact between the decisions made far up in the corporate hierarchy, and the learners who are the ultimate subjects of any fallout from those decisions. Because of this, it is often at the last minute and in the middle of a course when these sorts of conflict arise.

Content vs. Learner. Another form of content-oriented dilemmas are those situations in which the particular content in the required training regimen is not a good fit with the particular learners in the classroom. In a qualitative study some years back, a school teacher shared that she was forced to sit through an 8-hour class on how to help her students use iPads in the classroom. This was a meaningful experience for half of the teachers because they were issued iPads for the children in their classrooms, but the teacher I was talking to was in the half who did not have the devices, nor did they have the means to acquire them any time soon. That class was simply a very bad fit for half of the learners in it. Given how busy everyone is in the workplace and how many demands are placed against employees, this sort of a "forced" waste of time can generate quite a bit of frustration and even open hostility in the training room. The conscientious trainer is going to struggle with these sorts of dynamics.

Some training professionals are permitted the space to adjust on-the-fly while teaching and so can adjust for this sort of problem. Others, however, are tightly controlled by the rules of their particular training division and must roll forward with predetermined content exactly as it is. These situations bring the instructor quickly into the realm of experiencing an ethical dilemma.

Instructor Values vs. the Learner

Beyond all of these professional issues that can develop between the training professional and supervisors and training content, learners themselves can often present problems. Personality conflicts can be a very significant problem for the motivationally immediate instructor, because when a teacher is working to be motivationally immediate, learners are given space to express themselves in the classroom as part of the content, and part of the learning process. This can open the proverbial can of worms when there are those in the classroom who may be loud, overly assertive, prideful, and yes, sometimes even obnoxious.

During these moments, the instructor is forced to make a tough decision. Should one press on and use classroom management strategies to handle the different personalities, or revert back to the comfort of backing off, boxing learners out, and simply talking the content *at* them. Next slide please. *Click.*

Facilitator as Mediator (FAM): A Possible Way Forward

Before discussing the facilitator as a mediator, it is worth looking at a common alternative. One way of working through these difficulties is to see oneself as a negotiator. Seeing the instructional task as one of negotiating can be a very powerful way for a training professional to navigate the many conflicts mentioned above, because it allows the instructor to see teaching as a process by which the learning content must be negotiated with the learner, rather than simply one of transmitting content to the learner.

This view sees the instructor as a negotiator who has a set of considerations to bring before the learner (or perhaps the boss), with the purpose of getting as many through as possible and keeping their essence intact somehow in the process. This view has some power to it that the "sage-on-the-stage" approach lacks, because it assumes that the learner is not going to simply swallow everything spooned their way, and that a good teacher is one who engages in some form of work to win the buy-in of the learner. In my own earlier writing, I encouraged negotiation as a tactic.

However, it does very little to eliminate the ethical dilemmas above because it places the training professional in the place of being an active agent of the organization, and therefore being forced back into the same relative position the instructor had before adopting the mindset of negotiator in the first place. That is, it may resolve conflicts between the instructor and the learner but does not at all help the conflicts between the other parties listed above, such as the content itself or the training director or upper-level management.

This may sound odd because it is natural that a paid training professional who is also an employee of the organization, either directly or indirectly through contract would act in the interest of the employer. My point here is *not* to suggest that an instructor should be disloyal to the employer – that would simply be to suggest an additional ethical dilemma. What I am suggesting, however, is a *mindset* that will assist in easing some of the tensions and stand-stills caused by the dilemmas listed above.

A better approach is one that sees the facilitator as a mediator rather than a negotiator. Seeing the FAM, rather than negotiator, can be a useful way to work through these conflicts, if not eliminate them.[2] Unlike a negotiator, a mediator is someone who is not typically aligned with one side or the other but is assigned the task of making the two ends meet. And, unlike an arbiter, or arbitrator, a mediator does not have the ultimate authority to force an agreement. This is more closely aligned with the workplace training scenario than one might, at first, think. The training professional can neither force a supervisor to give-in to the instructional demands, nor can the training professional force an employee learner to learn anything at all in the classroom – at least what would be considered *effectual learning*.

A full read of the earlier academic work[3] on this will fill out the entire picture and the literature it is rooted in, but a brief explanation is provided here because adopting this type of thinking can assist the training professional in working in the space between the management and employee learners, between the content and the learner, between the learner and the learner, and even between the instructor and the instructor, all without being disloyal to either party.

The FAM concept is unique in at least three ways.[4] First, it focuses on the training professional's need to negotiate it two different directions, with two different parties, both of which are more powerful than the trainer – upper management, and the learners. Second, FAM addresses learning resistance and engagement, and it is these dynamics that cause the learner to be in the ultimate power position in the training context. The third is that FAM relies on very fluid, "boots on the ground" real-time interaction with learners during training sessions.

The negotiator "model" would have the training instructor, negotiating with the learners on behalf of the supervisors, which means that the positional space between what is supposed to be taught, and what learners are willing to buy-in to, is divided between the instructor and the learner. But, sometimes the learners have a legitimate reason to not like the training content, and, given the way training content is often determined, this will happen. It is also entirely possible for the instructor to have a problem with the content that they are required to teach. In other words, they think it is not that great either.

When the instructor or trainer directly ends up disagreeing with the employer (i.e., training content), then there is positional space that must be navigated in the other direction between the training professional and the member of management. It is this tension, from two different directions, that can create an ethical tension field. Clearly, the instructor doesn't want to just abandon the training content and be subversive, but to teach others to do something that either doesn't work, or creates a safety risk, doesn't seem right either. All expert instructors are also very protective of their classroom integrity and credibility because it is one of the most significant sources of success in that domain.

In these cases, the training professional can set aside the negotiator mindset and adapt that of a mediator. This seems like a subtle shift that would not have a substantial impact, but it does. First, as a mediator, the training professional can approach the member of management who made the initial training determination, and, instead of doing so as the idealistic opponent, they can do so as the concerned mediator who is professionally aware that although the employee learners may pass a test, effectual learning is very unlikely to occur.

In this sense, the mediator professional is simply sharing the reasons (and concern) that particular aspects of the training content will very likely be acquired (known) but *not* accepted (bought-in to). Given this, professional instructors being asked to train employees a certain way, would be on reasonable grounds to talk through these issues with the supervisor, to find out what suggestions the supervisor may have for what should be done about this.

Certainly, the supervisor may then just say "get it done," but the chances of having a meaningful discourse about it are greatly improved when it is not the instructor against the boss, but the instructor sharing the mindset of the learners with the boss, and also using professional concepts such as effectual learning (acquisition and acceptance) as the objective in order for training transfer to occur. Saying "I don't like this" is different from saying "the employees are not going to buy this for these reasons, which will negatively affect our workplace in the following ways…"

On the other end of the mediation, as the instructor is in the classroom with the employee learners, there are traditionally two choices. First, the instructor can just talk the slide, share the content that they don't professionally agree with. This is problematic for a number of reasons, chief among them that it can be ethically challenging to do so, and that it is highly unlikely that the learners are actually going to end up with effectual learning, which means that there will not be training transfer.

Second, the instructor can just be subversive and either skip the content, or trash-talk the content. I have heard so many times over the years (as both an instructor and a trainee) "Look, I don't want to be here and you don't either. You don't agree with this stuff and I don't either. Let's just get this done and go home." This, of course, has the exact same two problems as the first option – it has ethical implications, and the learners are not going to have effectual learning. This sort of training is most certainly a waste of resources because everyone in the room including the instructor have agreed right at the outset that it is not worth actually doing in the workplace.

The FAM option would have the training instructor – acting as a mediator between the upper management person who decided to include the controversial bit of content, and the employee learner who is simply not going to buy-it – talking with the employee learners about the content, why the management has decided it is necessary (which the instructor would now know), and under what circumstances the learners think it could work.

Likely, the employee learners would point out all of the reasons it is a problem, but this a good thing, given what we know about motivational immediacy. Only at this point is the instructor really drawing out the learner, finding out what they are about (what they think and feel), and having meaningful conversations about how to follow the mandates in an effective way that is safe.

This likely sounds far too simple and optimistic, but it is not when one considers that effectual learning is not taking place much of the time anyway.

That is, they were not going to do what you're training them to do anyway. It won't get worse if you talk through all of the reasons with them and allow them to "ventilate."[5] The importance of conceptual frameworks, storylines, and dialogue discussed in Chapter 7 comes into focus here. All of this taken together speaks to the fact that allowing learners to dialogue, be heard and understood as well as being told and tested, will definitively increase the probability that the learners will both acquire and accept the content that you are teaching.

FAM then allows the training professional to mediate between the boss and the employee learner, with the interests of both ultimately in mind, and the instructor's own professional knowledge and ethics being brought to bear in a reasonable way. A key benefit would be that the positional space mentioned earlier is now one space with the instructor operating outside of it as a mediator between the desires of management in the form of content, and the learner, in terms of their own knowledge and existing attitudes and dispositions.

Added to this, motivational immediacy concepts would suggest that this dynamic will have the greatest likelihood of having the learner experience effectual learning, which is the desired end of both management and the instructor, and is best for everyone involved in the long-run. FAM brings about a subtle shift, but can have significant impact in the workplace training context. It will not, of course, solve all problems or resolve all ethical dilemmas. What it does do, is allow the training professional to act as a training professional who is actually trying to close the gap as best as possible between the employer's required training content, and the employee learner's willingness to engage and experience effectual learning (i.e., training transfer).

A Bit about These Dilemmas and Leadership

This is yet another intersection for leadership to come into play. The moment a training instructor sees the need and steps into the gap to mediate the space between the training content mandated by management, and the learning sensibilities of the employee learners (which is quite often borne from experience), the instructor becomes more than an instructor, becoming instead a leader in the workplace. A mere instructor does the job and gets the paycheck, but the instructor who would be a leader becomes a calming presence in the workplace, and is seen as a stable and reliable caretaker by both those who are in higher positions in the workplace as well as those who are learners in the classroom.

For those who are reading this as formal leaders in the workplace, there is a mandate for you here as well. You may not teach in a classroom and so, although reading this in a bemused sort of way, may not think it has much meaning for you. In some ways, however, this entire problem could be resolved if enough of those in formal leadership roles made the effort to sit down with those who teach in the workplace and simply listen. Listen to what they experience as instructional staff, listen to what they know of their learners' viewpoints, attitudes, and struggles. Listen to how the content being proffered may be the subject of a very different storyline, or perhaps many different storylines in the classroom and working spaces.

And, after listening fully and regularly, work to be the leader that you are and either change the problem areas of the learning content (and policies and procedures), or use your power of persuasion to bring everyone else together to a place of having a mutually shared vision for the future. There is space here for everyone to step up and lead in their own way, and that is where the power of one's leadership extends its reach – by fostering authentic and meaningful leadership from everyone else around you.

Notes

1 Frye, S., Taylor, J., & Stafford, A. (2017). The first fifteen minutes: Learning engagement, learning resistance, and the impact of initial teacher-student contact. In C. X. Wang (Ed.), *Theory and practice of adult and higher education* (pp. 340, 342). Information Age Publishing.
2 Taylor, J. E. (2010). Facilitator as mediator: A content-related model of program development and delivery. *Adult Learning Quarterly*, *21*(1–2), 19–25.
3 Taylor, J. E. (2010). Facilitator as mediator: A content-related model of program development and delivery. *Adult Learning Quarterly*, *21*(1–2), 19–25.
4 Taylor, J. E. (2010). Facilitator as mediator: A content-related model of program development and delivery. *Adult Learning Quarterly*, *21*(1–2), 19–25.
5 Mitchell, G. (1988). *The trainer's handbook: The AMA guide to effective training* (3rd ed., p. 45). AMACON American Management Association.

Chapter 13

Reach

The Challenge

The challenge that comes along with the message shared in these pages is not so much to do different things, but to think in different ways. I have mentioned the word courage a number of times and it sometimes does come down to having courage enough to do something that we know to do. And, in truth, if there is anything that takes more courage than to do something, it is that required to *be* something.

Doing something connotes a somewhat temporary state of affairs, one that will have an end, and from which respite and reconsideration might be available. We can usually find many reasons to avoid doing that something again if it didn't turn out well because our commitment was limited to begin with. We followed through; we did it. Now we are done.

Becoming something on the other hand is a very different sort of commitment. It is a long-term commitment to a life of daily discipline, focused determination, and most likely routine adversity. This sort of commitment, however, is the everyday stuff of leaders everywhere and it is why, in the end, most of us follow them into the storm. The point of making the commitment is not to get everyone to follow into the storm. Storms will ultimately come – they always do. The commitment is made by the leader, and the line is held, so that we may lead everyone *out* when the time comes.

This language may fairly seem a bit dramatic for a book about leading, mentoring, and training in the workplace, and it may be. A marriage counselor once said at a speaking engagement that "life is lived in the mundane" and this is true of the workplace also. Nothing requires more sustained courage than facing the mundane and being the reason those around you don't see it as such. There is no storm more devastating than the mundane, and it is the leaders among us who distract us from noticing.

Human learning is not a simple, clinical, acquisition of rote technical detail, and the workplace training programs we try to harness it within can't

DOI: 10.4324/9781003482079-16

be the purveyance of it. Seeing human learning in different ways, understanding the true nature of motivation and how it works for and, quite often against us, and living in a disciplined state of motivational immediacy inside and out, will take work. It will take work, but it will extend our reach, increase the draw others feel around us, and unite those in your workplace around a common vision that has a durability that the rote acquisition of information will never have.

Always Look to See the Underneath

There are branches and there are root systems, and everyone knows which are in it for the long haul. None of us have awoken after a storm to find root systems scattered across our lawns (okay, I am sure someone has). Removing branches, however, is as routine a part of Saturday mornings for some people as golf is for others. So often in our training programs we focus on bending branches left and right, trying to stake them down in other areas only to find that they don't look good there either. Motivational Immediacy is about seeing the underneath of the thing – what is the essence. It is about seeing the root systems in your areas of practice, carefully deciding whether they are good, and then, if not, either digging them up and moving them, or getting rid of them altogether. It is a bottom-up system of thinking and, like most lasting things, starting with the foundation is the only good way to begin.

The way this works out in practice is to spend more time thinking about what human learning requires in your situation – what the people need and who they are – than changing the color of the slides in your presentation or using AI assistance to create a new image. Branches come and go. It is the roots that are there when the dust settles. Take the time necessary to plant the trees in the right place to begin with and pay attention to any that might need to be moved, no matter the effort required.

This is true of resistance in the classroom as well. An assertive learner may be trying to cause you problems or thwart the progress of everyone. Or an assertive learning might be the only one paying attention to what you are really saying. That learner might, in fact, be your only friend in the effort to make your workplace a better place. Take the time to find out where the roots lie. We only see what we look for. Look to see the underneath.

Join Your SME-ness

I brought up the term SME earlier in Chapter 9, the curriculum chapter, but am bringing it up here in its' positive sense. The idea of the subject matter expert can be a powerful tool if used in the right way. This makes it much like any other tool in that most can be damaging if misused or misunderstood. The traditional view of SMEs as they relate to the classroom instructor specifically, is the guru who knows what needs to be taught. The learners, on the other hand, in contrast to this, are blank slates to be written on, a tabula rasa for the instructor.

The problem with this common view is the false dichotomy it creates. Of course, we know that the learner is likely a SME about something, just not the topic at hand. This is true in a sense but remembering that teaching is a people skill – it is about the person – the content itself is only as good as how it gets encoded in the other. That is, it is always a construction of the material in the mind of the learner, not the simple transmission of it from a knower to a learner. If we are going for deep, authentic, conceptual, storyline knowing for the learner (the only kind that will result in consistent, long-term application and transfer), then the learner is an *equal* participant in the process.

This sort of collaboration is not the type we normally throw around, which is a trendy word game that shows us "up to date" and "with it," and makes the learner feel good (or, really probably just the person using the term). This sort of collaboration is a true collaboration. All teaching and learning always is. In this very real sense, the learner is also a subject matter expert about the teaching–learning experience you are trying to facilitate as an instructor. We tend to think of teaching and learning as being a somewhat one-dimensional transaction. Remember that knowing something is about the something and teaching something to someone is about the someone. Because of this empirical fact, the teaching–learning field is much more complicated. It includes the content, but also the conceptual framework and storyline of the instructor, the conceptual framework and storyline of the learner, the local and extended context and culture of the workplace, and the psychological and sociological inner workings (and baggage) of both the instructor and the learner. This is one of the reasons that an instructor truly is a facilitator, notwithstanding the word games we play with that term.

When this dynamic is seen with its complex and cluttered field, it becomes clear that when considering only content, the instructor, not the learner, is the SME. But when taking a look at the learning dynamic, which has content as only one equally weighted factor, it is clear that the learner is a SME with every bit the authenticity, power, and importance of the instructor. It is the job then of the instructor when teaching (and leader when leading) to facilitate the joining together of these two domains of expertise. This final chapter opened with a call to think in different ways, and this is a clear example of that in practice. See the process differently. See the SME in every individual learner you encounter and work to join your SMEness.

Teach like a Leader and Lead Like a Teacher

There are clearly differences between teaching and leading when one looks at them on the whole. Academically, we could spend quite a bit of time splitting hairs over which is connected to the other (or not), in what ways, and with what implications. I have worked to avoid that in this book largely because getting to the bottom of that question would have limited effect on practice. Instead, I have tried to stay in the clear with concepts and relationships that are somewhat easy to see for most everyone. And, more than anything, the point is not to demonstrate that they are the same, but to help those who would do either, hope to do both instead.

Most often, those who see themselves as leaders work to influence others in all of the human-centered, nuanced ways that rely on charisma, competence, and reliability. They are fully aware that it is a people skill. Teaching and training, however, are seen as something other, something cold, clinical, and ostensibly scientific. Leaders can fail to tap into the huge wealth of knowledge on how human beings are influenced to begin with, how they change their conceptual frameworks and form their storylines, and, most importantly, how they interpret everything the leader does through those two things.

Instructors, on the other hand, often see leading as something different and outside of their own practice and focus instead on conveying the rote acquisition of knowledge to some other learning sponge, thinking little of whether or not the learner actually agrees, buys-in, and changes their whole way of being for the long-term. Our tests and assessments have made this a comfortable space to teach in. In this sense, trainers often don't take the job as seriously as it really is. In this way, both leaders and instructors often view learning the same way.

The call here is to see teaching in all cases and in all ways as a space for providing powerful, influential leadership to others in a way that results in the entire workplace community having the same clear shared vision. Teach like a leader and by all means, lead like a teacher.

Reach For

At the heart of all of this is a proposal to be intentional in all that we do in the world of leading, mentoring, and teaching in the workplace. We are, in fact, both teaching and leading at all places and at all times, whether we like it or not. These dynamics are a reality of the working life, which is like all other human enterprises – deeply social. We cannot always change what is, but we can always change how we respond to what is. Motivational immediacy is about keeping before us at all times, the goals we have for our unit, our division, our workplace, and our life. If motivational immediacy is to be as powerful as it can be, it must be bone deep, not a piece of jewelry we put on in the morning before work.

These habits are cultivated at home first, and then at work. The call to *reach for* should not be taken as a mandate to cast aside all enjoyable moments of the present in view of some distant hope for the future. It is, in fact, the opposite. The best enjoyment of the present moment will always come with the abiding hope for the future, and it is only when we know who we are and what we want that we can justify taking the time off to rest and play. It is only then, that we will be able to enjoy all the moments of our lives as true pleasures rather than guilty ones.

We can be sticks in a stream, bumping along with the current, maybe surging ahead, or maybe caught up instead in the debris on the side. Or, we can act with the purest form of dignity and be purposeful in what we do and how we do it. You have already been engaged in some motivational immediacy if you are reading this book, even more if you have finished it. What you get out of it will be firmly connected to what you have put into it. Reach.

Index

Note: Figures are indicated by *italics* and tables are in **bold** type.

For Product Safety Concerns and Information please contact our EU representative GPSR@taylorandfrancis.com
Taylor & Francis Verlag GmbH, Kaufingerstraße 24, 80331 München, Germany

www.ingramcontent.com/pod-product-compliance
Ingram Content Group UK Ltd.
Pitfield, Milton Keynes, MK11 3LW, UK
UKHW020650121225
465993UK00022B/1953

* 9 7 8 1 0 3 2 7 6 4 3 9 9 *